BISHOPS
ON THE BORDER
Pastoral Responses to Immigration

Mark Adams, Minerva G. Carcaño,
Gerald Kicanas, Kirk Smith,
and Stephen Talmage

Morehouse Publishing
NEW YORK · HARRISBURG · DENVER

Morehouse Publishing, 4775 Linglestown Road, Harrisburg, PA 17112
Morehouse Publishing, 19 East 34th Street, New York, NY 10016
Morehouse Publishing is an imprint of Church Publishing Incorporated.

www.churchpublishing.org

Cover design by Laurie Klein Westhafer
Typeset by Denise Hoff

Library of Congress Cataloging-in-Publication Data

A catalog record of this book is available from the Library of Congress.

ISBN-13: 978-0-8192-2875-8 (pbk.)
ISBN-13: 978-0-8192-2876-5 (ebook)

Printed in the United States of America

Contents

— human rds struggle of our time

— walk in solidarity w/ those
who were surely the poorest
of the poor + marginalized

— indigenous

— Why politics... money... war... violence

— not defiance, but the
simple human struggle for
survival

iii

Foreword

The spark that ignited this book project was a conversation I had with the best-selling author Diana Butler Bass in the coffee shop of the Phoenix airport about two years ago. I had requested some time in her busy schedule for help on another writing project of mine, and I was fortunate that she was able to work me in during a layover between speaking engagements. At the end of our conversation, she turned to me and said. "You know, those of us in the pews are really curious about what you bishops are thinking. We only see official (and boring) policy papers. What we would really like to know is what shapes your faith? What makes you tick? I know you are all busy with church administration, but why don't you write more? With the exception of John Spong [the controversial retired Episcopal Bishop of Newark], I am not aware of any bishops (at least in the Episcopal Church) who are publishing."

I took her words as a personal challenge, and on my way back to the airport parking lot, it occurred to me that my bishop colleagues and I were all deeply preoccupied by a challenge that had huge implications for our churches and for our country. None of us had any quick fix for the immigration crisis, and none of us were scholarly enough to explain its historical and political roots, but all of us had witnessed pain and suffering on the border up close, and we knew its face, a face we tried to share with others.

And so I put these questions to my colleagues. "How has your involvement in the immigration struggle changed your soul?" And "would you be willing to share publicly how it has changed you?" I am profoundly grateful for their answers and for their willingness to share some of their deepest thoughts that form the heart of this little book.

Growing up in a white, middle-class, Christian family during the 1960s meant that I was surrounded by images of the civil rights movement. My parents were shocked by photographs of black protesters facing fire hoses and snarling attack dogs in the streets of Birmingham and were galvanized by the speeches of Martin Luther King Jr. My father was the administrative leader of the Presbyterian Church in Arizona; my mother was seminary-educated and wrote children's Sunday school curricula. They joined with other local progressive clergy of many different denominations to rally support for the cause, not always easy to do in the conservative political climate of Phoenix, Arizona. My brother and I wore little buttons to school with a white equal sign printed on a black background, which caused us to be shoved into the lockers of our junior high school or to be called "nigger lovers" by our classmates.

My family was politically and intellectually on the side of those struggling for freedom and dignity in our American South. The only problem was that I had never known a black person or experienced what it was like to be on the receiving end of racism. It wasn't until I was a senior in high school that there was a black student in our school, nor did I have a close African-American friend until far later, in graduate school. For me, notions of freedom, liberty, and equality were intellectual concepts, ideals to be embraced by all right-thinking Americans. As a product of a privileged and reasonably affluent upbringing, I had no experience of the corrosive power of prejudice and discrimination to poison communities and destroy souls. I knew about suffering, but I had never been there.

That changed for me one summer when I attended a church camp. Our counselor felt that his white-skinned twelve-year-olds would benefit from hearing what it was like to grow up as a black person and so he asked a friend of his to come talk to us over the course of several days. I will never forget watching her face as she shared with us her memories of being subjected to insults and abuse as a young person. Though she tried to keep her tone light and a smile on her face, in the course of her narrative, a tear formed in her eye and gradually trickled down her cheek. She never wiped it away. That tear has long remained in my mind as an image of the evil of racial oppression. I don't remember the woman's name, but I will be forever grateful to her for putting a face on the effects of prejudice.

Years later I was to have a similar experience of "putting a face on oppression" as I spent time with those whose lives and families were being shaped by the hatred they experienced as they attempted to enter this country in search of a better life. I learned once again that there is a huge chasm between simply knowing about suffering and experiencing it firsthand; between seeing it portrayed in the media, and living it; between embracing the theological and moral imperatives to love our neighbor, and being part of that neighbor's life.

As a clergyperson, and as a bishop, I was especially sensitive to my need to "practice what you preach." I knew enough of the Bible to know that Jesus's harshest words of condemnation were not directed against those guilty of moral failures or even harmful excesses, but against those religious leaders who preached godliness, but who were unable to respond to actual human suffering when it was right before them. Such were the leaders who have that most chilling of all dialogues with Jesus at the end of the Gospel of Matthew, asking him incredulously, "Lord, when did we see thee hungry . . . ?"

I also knew that I was not the only one of my colleagues feeling this tension. One of the great pleasures of working

in Arizona has been the opportunity to form close colle-
gial connections with other religious leaders. The Arizona
Ecumenical Council has been around since the 1960s, when
it was founded by a group of bishops and executives from
most of the mainline churches (including my own father
when he was the synod executive for the United Presbyterian
Church in Arizona). Under the leadership of its director, the
Rev. Jan Flaaten, it has been an outspoken voice on social
justice issues for more than a decade. Monthly "BERT"
lunches (Bishop and Executive Round Tables) have allowed
us to form a deep personal fellowship and share our hopes
and dreams.

Four of us were drawn together by our involvement in
border and immigration issues. Some, like United Methodist
bishop Minerva Carcaño (a Latina by birth) and Tucson
Roman Catholic bishop Gerald Kicanas, both fluent Spanish
speakers, had long been involved with the pastoral and legal
needs of their Hispanic congregations. Lutheran (ELCA)
bishop Steve Talmadge and I were newer to the debate, but
we both had spent much of our lives in Arizona and were
familiar with its often strange brew of rugged individualism
and reactionary politics.

We all realized that what was needed in the nationwide
discussion over illegal immigration was for people to get
to know one another as people and not as political issues.
"Putting a face on immigration" was something we all had
attempted to do in our own ministries.

The format of this offering is simple: to share with you
a part of our "spiritual autobiography" as it relates to our
experience working on the Arizona border, the geographic
flash point for the immigration debate. Our approach is
to be personal and confessional, which means that we also
have, in places, made ourselves vulnerable. We expect criticism. We have all experienced it in heavy doses over the last
decade. I have received far more hate-mail (and to be fair,
also many complimentary letters) for positions I have taken

on immigration than on any other actions that I have ever taken as a bishop. I know that my coauthors have also experienced verbal abuse, and even threats of physical violence. It also should be pointed out that all of our contributions are written from the heart, not from the head. None of us are social scientists; rather we are "chief pastors" trying to care for a part of our flocks and those outside our flocks, whom we see in pain. However, in order to set the stage for our personal narratives, we asked the Rev. Mark Adams, a young bilingual Presbyterian clergyman who has lived on the border for many years, and who is known and respected by all of us, to provide an introduction to help our readers better understand some of the complex historical and political realities in which we have been working.

Since we began this project, there have been many changes in the immigration debate. The political realities are different than they were just two years ago. Even though we have done our best to keep our own narratives current, we are aware that our experiences are only a snapshot in time of an unfolding historical process. It should also be said that given the changed political environment and improving economic conditions in Mexico, as well as shifting power structures evident in our own 2012 elections in this country, we all are feeling more hopeful that our country will address the immigration crisis in a more productive and humane way in the near future. Indeed, even as this book goes to press, there are signs that Congress might overcome political differences and finally address comprehensive immigration reform. Still, the fundamental issues of hatred and injustice will not be solved overnight.

A wise old priest once used this metaphor when it came to describing his church's involvement in controversial issues of social justice. "Our job as clergy is not to tell engineers how to build a bridge, but to remind them that the existing one is dangerous and needs to be rebuilt." Hence we hope that our contribution is neither partisan nor polemical but rather prophetic, using our own stories to bring attention to an issue that has rightly been called the "civil and human rights struggle of our time." Just like the clergy I saw in television and magazine images during my childhood, their black suits and clergy collars making them immediately identifiable, my colleagues and I have no political agenda in writing this book. We do, however, share their moral agenda to stand in solidarity with those who struggle for human dignity. We believe that task is one that far transcends our denominational differences and that unites us under the God-given imperative to care for the stranger—the alien—in our midst. We have different ideas as to how Christians might do this, but we are absolutely agreed that this is the Great Commandment that Jesus has given us.

The fact that we are all bishops gives us, and perhaps our readers, a different perspective. In one of the important treatises of the early church, the *Letter to the Smyrnaeans* of St Ignatius of Antioch (d. ca. 108), we read "where the bishop is, there let the people be." The office of leadership God has entrusted to us is more than that of chief executive officer or public relations spokesperson of our respective denominations. For better or worse, we are the symbolic expressions of the apostolic mission that has been handed on to us by Jesus's earliest disciples. The Greek root of the word *apostolic* means "sent." Christians have always been sent, like Jesus, to serve those who are poor and marginalized. Our presence on the border of our country is where we believe Jesus directs us to be. It is not our mission, but his. We invite the rest of the church to join us there.

Kirk Smith

Acknowledgments

We have all agreed on one simple acknowledgment: to those men, women, and children on both sides of our border who struggle to support their families and whose faith and perseverance in the face of enormous suffering has been an inspiration to us all. To them we dedicate this book, as we also dedicate any profits it might make to their support.

Introduction

Mark Adams

The church of the U.S./Mexico borderlands has been in a unique position to witness to the growing division, fear, and death occurring on our shared border as well as in the interiors of our nations. It is in this context of tension and suffering that we are called to bear witness to the good news of Jesus Christ who "is our peace; in his flesh he has made both groups into one and has broken down the dividing wall, that is, the hostility between us" (Ephesians 2:14).

Being part of the church that crosses national, political, social, linguistic, and cultural borders has enabled us to experience the suffering on both sides of the border—whether it is crying with family members in Mexico who have lost loved ones in the deserts or listening to the frustration of property owners in the United States who have lost a sense of physical and financial security because of persons crossing through their property; whether celebrating in worship with migrants who give witness to how God saved their lives again or praying with Border Patrol agents who sometimes fear for their safety; or grieving with families on both sides of the border as they struggle with the violence of an underground drug culture. Because we are in relationship with people on multiple sides of the "issues" and have become familiar with the realities and complexity of the situation, it has become impossible for us to scapegoat any group of people.

In fact, the border reality has given greater insight into what the Scripture means when it says "our struggle is not against enemies of blood and flesh but against the rulers, against the authorities, against the cosmic powers of this present darkness, against the spiritual forces of evil in the heavenly places" (Ephesians 6:12). We seek to raise awareness that our struggle is not against individuals or any particular group of individuals, but rather against political, economic, and social systems that pit individuals against one another and promote division instead of unity, fear instead of hope, death instead of life. By pitting undocumented persons against ranchers or "coyotes" against Border Patrol agents, we understand that those with power benefit the most while the ones who currently suffer the most are the undocumented and the property owners.

As Christians we are called to work together across national boundaries and to address our common concerns as sisters and brothers equally created in the divine image. We are not adversaries. Furthermore, we are called to resist the temptation to demonize or dehumanize any individual or group of individuals. By building relationships and understanding across borders, those most affected by the current policies can unite to struggle for change that is beneficial to people on both sides of the border.

Bishops on the Border provides a wonderful source of biblical and theological reflection on the practice of the Christian faith from four different expressions of the body of Christ working and living within the sociopolitical and economic realities of the early twenty-first-century U.S./Mexico borderlands. The bishops challenge not only their own communions, but all of us who call upon the name of Christ to respond in faith rather than fear to the complexity of migration. As we respond to the challenges of today, we are called to remember both our biblical history and our corporate history. My colleague Tommy Bassett has a phrase that he attaches to his e-mails: "Are we there yet? Are you kidding? WE ARE NOMADS!" As people of faith, we are reminded that we are pilgrims and sojourners on this earth and our faith story is filled with people on the move. Migration is as old as Adam and Eve. Our ancestors migrated from their homelands for as many reasons as people today migrate: from political and economic necessities to religious and family concerns.[1] The story of our foremothers and forefathers in the faith is part of the larger reality of migration in the context of human history, but there was no such thing as immigration until the development, rather late in human history, of sociopolitical borders and the division of God's creation into nation states. With the development of national borders, the migration of peoples entailed not just internal migration borders, but also the reality of emigration from, and immigration to, other countries. While we often focus on the reality of the migration of peoples, it is also important for us to remember that not only do people migrate, but borders and policies also migrate.

The Migration of Borders

There is a fence between Douglas, Arizona, and its twin city of Agua Prieta, Sonora, Mexico, where I live and have been in ministry since 1998—one year after this fence was built.

Imagine that you are standing with your back against the south side of that fence, looking toward the southern border of Mexico and Guatemala. Where would you be standing? Now, it is the United States, because the fence is built a little more than a foot north of the international boundary marker that divides the United States from Mexico. With your back up against the fence, you would be 100 percent in the United States—unless you have very long feet or a very large belly.

---

1   Adam and Eve were expelled from the Garden of Eden (Genesis 3); Noah and his family were displaced because of the flood (Genesis 6); Abram and Sarai left their country to follow the call of God (Genesis 12); Joseph was sold into slavery and forcibly taken to Egypt (Genesis 37); Joseph's brothers go to Egypt because of famine (Genesis 42); and this is just a few examples from the first book of the Penteteuch.

But let's transport ourselves back over six hundred years to the year 1400. If you were in that same spot in the year 1400, where would you be standing? You would be standing in a place where the concept of nation states had not yet developed. You would be in "First Nations land" or indigenous territory, before the arrival of people from Europe. The ancestors of the Opata and the Pima peoples who inhabited the area had migrated there years before.

Now let's imagine you are still standing in the same location and are transported to 1550. Where would we be standing? According to traditional Western European cartography, you would now be standing in New Spain. However, the Opata and Pima who inhabited the region would have not known it as such and the area still had little exposure to persons of European descent. One of the early European "immigrants" to the area, Father Eusebio Francisco Kino, a Jesuit missionary, called the high desert region just west of here *La Pimería Alta*. We could say that the land was contested, not fully under the control of the Spanish powers as of yet.

Now let's transport ourselves to 1821. Where are we now? Mexico? First Nations land? Or contested land? In European terms, it was now known as Mexico. Mexico had fought its War for Independence from 1810 to 1821, so from the point of view of many south of here, this land was Mexican. After the Mexican-American War was fought from 1846 to 1848, the Treaty of Guadalupe Hidalgo established the border between the two countries close to where it is today, but not exactly. So where would we be standing if we were standing here in 1848? Answer: Mexico! This part of the country did not become part of the United States of America until after the Gadsden Purchase in 1854, when the land south of the Gila River and west of the Rio Grande became part of the United States. The land under our feet first became New Mexico Territory, then Arizona Territory, and then, in 1912, the state of Arizona.

Because of the migration of these borders, we have a variety of people from European, indigenous, and other backgrounds in a place that itself has experienced the migration of its own political borders. There are people of Mexican and Spanish descent in the Southwest who say, "We didn't cross the border; the border crossed us." Why do borders migrate? Politics . . . money . . . war. . . . It is not usually a peaceful or democratic process. Violence is often a part of the migration of borders. This is an important part of our corporate story; unfortunately, the church has often been complicit in the violence perpetuated in the migration of borders.

Jesus Gallegos, a Presbyterian pastor from Mexico, often says, in regard to the spread of the Christian faith, that the Catholics arrived with the cross in one hand, the sword in the other, and their pockets empty; the Protestants arrived with the Bible in one hand, a rifle in the other, and their pockets empty.

The Meaning and Implications of Borders Migration

The meaning and implications of borders migrate as well. The political, cultural, demographic, and economic context of our nation always determines the meaning and implications of our borders. The border between the United States and Mexico has a very different meaning with starkly different implications in 2013 than it did when its most recent demarcation was set by the Gadsden Purchase over 150 years ago. When the border between the United States and Mexico was finalized in the 1850s, it was a political border that marked where the spheres of influence and power of the United States and Mexico began and ended. It was not designed to prevent people of Mexican descent from crossing back and forth to see their families on the other side or vice versa. It was not a border designed to keep commerce from going back and forth.

For over sixty years, there was no federal armed presence on our southern border. In 1906, the United States had sent a group of armed folks into Mexico, at the request of Porfirio Diaz, the longtime dictator, to put down a strike. Diaz's action allowing foreign armed intervention into Mexico to support the economic interests of foreign capitalists over the interest of Mexican workers provided some of the early sparks to the Revolution. Our government placed the first armed military presence on the U.S. southern border in 1915 during the Mexican Revolution, which by that time had turned into a civil war. The U.S. government sent troops to Douglas, Arizona, to "hold the line" during the Second Battle of Agua Prieta and to keep the violence from seeping over the border.

The Mexican Revolution was successful in deposing Porfirio Diaz, who fled the country. After he fled, another civil war flared up, as factions of the Revolution sparred for power. Pancho Villa led one faction and Vanustiano Carranza led another. The United States had pledged neutrality, but as the fighting approached the border, eventually the U.S. government had to decide which side it would support. Pancho Villa planned to arrive in Agua Prieta, so as Pancho Villa headed there, Carranza contacted the Wilson administration and asked the United States for two things: 1) to allow his troops to cross U.S. territory to get to Agua Prieta, and 2) to send troops from El Paso to Douglas to back up his troops in Agua Prieta. The U.S. government said yes to both requests, and from that point on, Pancho Villa became our enemy. General John Pershing and Pancho Villa, once pictured hugging each other, became mortal enemies. Villa was soundly defeated at Agua Prieta, where Plutarco Elias Calles, later president of Mexico, led the reinforced troops.

During the Revolution, many battles took place in the northern regions of Mexico, and many families and individuals fled to the United States to escape the violence. Our military presence at the border did not, nor was it designed to, keep families from crossing the border as they sought refuge from the war and the economic devastation that it brought.

The U.S. Border Patrol, the first civilian law enforcement agency designed to control our borders, was not founded until 1924, 148 years after the Declaration of Independence and 70 years after the Gadsden Purchase was finalized. In that year, there were only two Border Patrol offices: El Paso and Detroit. In the 1920s, our nation was in the midst of Prohibition. Part of the purpose of our new Border Patrol was to keep illegal drugs (in a liquid form) from crossing the border. To this day, preventing illegal drugs from entering the United States continues to be one of the main goals of the U.S. Border Patrol. The Border Patrol was also intended to enforce the Chinese Exclusion Act—the first exclusionary immigration act, passed by the U.S. Congress in 1882.

In October of 1929, the socioeconomic and political context began to change dramatically with the stock market crash and the onset of the Great Depression. The 1930s brought the first mass deportation of people from the United States back to Mexico. This deportation, however, affected more than people who were Mexican citizens who had crossed the U.S./Mexico border to live and work in the United States. U.S. citizens of Mexican descent from families whom the border had crossed were also caught up in the raids and were deported along with thousands of Mexican citizens who had crossed the border when the meaning of that border did not include fear of deportation.

The Migration of Policies

The Second World War ushered in another dramatic cultural and economic shift in the United States. During the early 1940s, the economy of the United States boomed as our government mobilized "to save the world from fascism."

U.S. participation in World War II so increased U.S. economic vitality that this country was the only major combatant to emerge from the war economically stronger than it had been before.

The labor market that fueled U.S. economic expansion during the 1940s also experienced dramatic changes. Much of the traditional male labor force joined the armed forces and went to war while women entered the labor market in substantial numbers for the first time to supply workers for our war production. Our history books seldom mention another group who entered the U.S. workforce during that period in large numbers—male laborers from Mexico. In 1942, the United States and Mexico agreed to permit the legal entry of large numbers of Mexican men to fill the demand for labor to keep our agricultural economy going. Officially known as the Mexican Farm Labor Program, it is more popularly known as the Bracero Program, from the Spanish word *brazos,* which means arms.

The Bracero Program was enacted by executive order and was intended to be a temporary program from 1942 to 1947. Yet, when the war was over and the GIs returned home, they did not go back into the fields. Hundreds of thousands went to college under the G.I. Bill, one of the most amazing pieces of legislation that our country has ever passed. These working class folks, who otherwise would never have had the opportunity for higher education, were granted the opportunity to go and study. So, to continue to fill the shortage in agricultural workers, the U.S. and Mexican governments extended the Bracero Program for another five years, and in 1951 the U.S. Congress formalized the program with the passage of Public Law 78.

By the 1960s, there were two large political forces in the United States that came together to end the Bracero Program. Organized labor was opposed to it because they were concerned that *braceros* took jobs from Americans and depressed wages. The other force was the civil rights movement. Civil rights groups argued that the Bracero Program was a legalized form of slavery that abused workers. Why would they say that?

Let me give you an example. Suppose I were a *bracero*, here from Mexico and working for "Mr. Smith," a grower, as a tomato picker. I could come into the country legally, but I could only work for Mr. Smith. I couldn't legally work for anyone else. I am documented to do exactly one thing—work for Mr. Smith. It's harvest time, and I bring in two thousand pounds of tomatoes and I take them to Mr. Smith and I say, "Señor, here are your tomatoes." Then, he says, "Oh, Mark, you are such a great tomato picker, and I'm so proud of you, but I have a problem. I haven't been paid for these tomatoes yet. Would it be OK if I paid you next week?" And I say, "Sure, that's OK, next week will be fine." I come back next week with another two thousand pounds of tomatoes. And Mr. Smith says, "That's wonderful; I got paid for last week's tomatoes, but I can only pay you for half of what I owe you for this week. I'll catch up next week."

And so it continued. There were growers who followed the rules, but lots of folks who didn't. So what do I do? Do I complain? What would happen if I do? The word would get out that I'm a problem worker, and Mr. Smith would try to send me back to Mexico. And if I left Mr. Smith's farm and tried to work for someone else, no one would hire me. Thousands of workers were never paid the wages they were owed, and their children and grandchildren have had to fight for their stolen wages. There were major abuses of farm laborers, and the federal government officially terminated the program in 1964.

The end of the Bracero Program did not stop people from crossing the border to look for work, nor did it end the desire of growers to have a reliable source of labor. In 1965, people did not have to risk their lives to come to the United States to work for Mr. Smith or the thousands of other growers throughout the country. Crossing was easy, even without papers, and many farm workers migrated to

California and the south, and then north, to follow the crops during the growing season. Some returned to Mexico when the last crops were harvested in the north, but many didn't, and the presence of undocumented persons of Mexican descent in the United States grew steadily.

Neither the Mexican government nor the U.S. government thought it was a good idea to have hundreds of thousands of unemployed Mexican men on the south side of the U.S./Mexico border because of the potential for revolution. Stability was in the best interest of both governments, and both countries were interested in developing a legal avenue for Mexican workers. In 1965, the U.S. government and the Mexican government developed the Border Industrialization Act, which created a kind of Free Trade Zone area all along the border. Under this act, U.S. companies could go to the border and build twin factories, one in Mexico, one in the United States. Factories on the Mexican side paid lower wages than the ones in the United States, but the wages were much higher than in the rest of Mexico at the time. Our two governments saw this as a win-win situation—a constant supply of jobs on both sides of the border and a ready source of labor for U.S. companies in Mexico.

The Border Industrialization Act was supposed to stimulate economic growth on both sides of the border. The towns on the Arizona/Sonoran border did experience a tremendous amount of growth between 1965 to the present, especially on the Mexican side of the border. The factories that were built, known as *maquiladoras,* were a huge magnet for migration to the north from other parts of Mexico.

The population growth began accelerating in the 1980s; since 1990, both Nogales and Agua Prieta, Sonora, have doubled in size from 107,936 to 220,292 and 39,120 to 79,138 respectively.[2] A large portion of that growth is

---

2 From census figures from the Instituto Nacional De Estadistica y Geografia, www.inegi.org.mx.

directly related to the migration of persons from the rural regions of Sonora and the poorer states of Mexico to work in the factories in the border towns.

By the mid-1980s, there were over 3 million persons with undocumented status in the United States. The Immigration Reform and Control Act of 1986 signed into law by President Ronald Reagan provided a pathway to legalization for persons who had entered the United States prior to 1982 and had maintained residence. In an attempt to prevent a magnet for future unauthorized migration, the law, for the first time, made it illegal for employers to hire persons who did not have legal authorization to work in the United States.

1994—The Nexus of Politics, Economics, and Immigration

In 1994, three critical events happened that have continued to shape and define U.S./Mexico relationships. The first was the North American Free Trade Agreement (NAFTA), which expanded the Border Industrialization Act from the southern border of Mexico all the way up to the Arctic. The governments of all three countries—Mexico, the United States, and Canada—worked hard to reach this agreement. The governments of all three nations saw NAFTA as "mutually beneficial" for the people of all three nations.

Second, on January 1, 1994, the day that NAFTA went into effect, the Zapatistas, a mainly indigenous group in Chiapas in the south of Mexico, rose up in rebellion against the Mexican government. There are over sixty official languages and indigenous groups recognized in the Mexican constitution, and the Zapatistas, a coalition of indigenous groups, believed that NAFTA would speed up the destruction of these indigenous cultures in several ways:

■ Land—From the days of independence through the Revolution, from 1821 to 1910, land had been concentrated in the hands of a few large landholders, but the Revolution had changed that. The Revolutionary cry was, "Tierra y Libertad"—Land and Freedom. Land was distributed to indigenous peoples and was precious to them. The constitution that emerged after the Revolution decreed that communal land could never be sold; this was to prevent history from repeating itself, to keep wealthy ranchers from grabbing tracts of land away from indigenous farmers. But to be able to participate in NAFTA, the United States required Mexico to change that part of its constitution. Communal land could now be sold. The Zapatistas fought against this change, but the government believed that it would help lead Mexico into the industrial age and create jobs outside of the small-farming agricultural sector,

- NAFTA required that Mexico remove tariffs on goods coming into Mexico from the United States and Canada. This profoundly affected Mexican agriculture, for under the free market arrangement, Mexico could no longer exclude the importation from the United States of commodities such as corn and soybeans, the mainstays of Mexican agriculture.

- NAFTA also required an end to agricultural subsidies to small farmers in Mexico while U.S. agricultural subsidies to its corn and soybean farmers have risen in the last sixteen years to $40 billion a year. This imbalance in subsidy practice is a sticking point each time the "developed" world and the so-called "developing" world sit down for trade negotiations Highly industrialized, highly productive, efficient, and highly subsidized U.S. and Canadian agribusiness is now in direct competition with nonsubsidized, subsistence farmers in Mexico, undercutting the prices of Mexican agricultural products. As a result, farmers in Mexico couldn't make it.

So 1994 was a pivotal year in Mexico: There was agricultural sector job loss as Mexico began removing subsidies and tariffs for imported agricultural goods in a phase-out that was completed in 2008. Although it was gradual, small farmers did not have enough time to adjust to the new competition. Since it was now possible to sell their land, farmers sold out and moved to the cities to find work. When there were not enough jobs in the cities close to their villages, they would often find their way north to the border factories. Once on the border, if there were not enough jobs or the possibility of making significantly higher wages in the United States was irresistible, many crossed the border to support their families.

In 1992, when Ross Perot ran for president, he had warned that if NAFTA were passed there would be a "giant sucking sound" of American jobs leaving the United States for Mexico. Textile jobs, for instance, had first gone from New England to places like Georgia and South Carolina, and then, with NAFTA, he predicted that they would go to Mexico. Although under NAFTA, some U.S. jobs migrated south and created a boom in the industrial sector in the north of Mexico, there was also a huge economic crisis in Mexican agriculture. Mexico lost more jobs in the agriculture sector in the 1990s than were gained in the industrial sector, and job growth as a whole did not keep up with the growth in the Mexican labor force. Meanwhile, job creation in the United States was focused in the service sector, providing lots of low-wage, relatively low-skill jobs to fill, exacerbating the push/pull that was already present in the border area.

In the early 1990s, the United States was coming out of a recession. Remember the catch phrase for the 1992 Clinton campaign? "It's the economy, stupid." The economy was in rough shape, and Clinton rode the wave of discontent into the White House. During the campaign, however, Pat Buchanan, a conservative Republican, emerged as a political voice. He went to San Diego and saw people crossing the border in huge numbers. He talked about the importance of securing our borders and stopping the "brown wave." He never became a political candidate, but his anti-immigrant arguments in the debate influenced all of the candidates, and Clinton became a great supporter of increasing border and immigration enforcement. At this same time, politically, the border underwent the largest transformation in our history, initiating the third critical event of 1994, Operation Gatekeeper.

Operation Gatekeeper began as a pilot program called Operation Hold-the-Line in El Paso, Texas, in 1993, when Border Patrol Chief Silvestre Reyes, said, "I can't stop people from crossing the border everywhere, but I can stop people from crossing right here in El Paso." He positioned his agents right on the border in a concentrated space, then behind them he placed more agents in the gaps behind the front line of agents. In football, this is called goal line defense. It worked very effectively to keep people from crossing the border at El Paso, and it worked politically. But migration then moved away from the cities, and individuals and families began crossing elsewhere . . . in the remote desert areas between the cities. The "goal" of El Paso was defended, but there were one thousand miles on either side until the sidelines.

In 1994, Operation Gatekeeper was carried out in San Diego/Tijuana to block migrants from coming through those cities as well as a way of responding to national anti-immigrant political trends. Unfortunately, the federal government initiated Operation Gatekeeper in the same year that the state of California passed Proposition 187, denying undocumented immigrants the benefits of education and health care.[3] This new policy of stopping migration at the border in highly populated areas and intentionally funneling the flow of migration to less populated areas became the practice all along the U.S./Mexico border. Operation Safeguard arrived in Arizona in 1996, and shortly thereafter, to the rest of Texas as

---

3 The federal courts eventually ruled Proposition 187 unconstitutional.

Operation Rio Grande. More and more border crossers were being forced into the desert, and the death toll began to rise.

With the signing of the Illegal Immigration Reform and Immigrant Responsibility Act of 1996,[4] President Clinton began a massive increase in the budget for border protection which included a mandate to double the number of Border Patrol Agents from under 5,000 in 1995 to 10,000 by 2001. The actual numbers ended up being 4,388 in 1995 to 9,147 by 2001.[5] During the same period, the annual budget for the U.S. Border Patrol increased from $452 million dollars to $1.146 billion dollars. Under the Bush and Obama administrations, we have continued the policy of increasing the budget and the number of Border Patrol agents. Currently, we have over 21,000 Border Patrol agents deployed—the vast majority along our southern border. The U.S. Border Patrol budget for FY 2011 was $4.6 billion.[6]

Unlike the Immigration Reform and Control Act signed by President Reagan in 1986[7] that provided a pathway to legalization for persons who were in the United States without authorization prior to the Act, Clinton's "reform" provided no such relief and only focused on the removal of persons in the United States without authorization and the deterrence of future undocumented immigrants.

Border "Control" and Its Consequences

For 150 years there had been a fluid border between U.S. and Mexico, but suddenly the border was being robustly

---

4   See http://www.visalaw.com/96nov/3nov96.html for a summary of law.
5   From U.S. Border Patrol Headquarters Public Affairs Office report, September 25, 2009.
6   http://blog.sfgate.com/nov05election/2010/02/01/obama-beefs-up-border-security-in-2011-budget.
7   http://www.uscis.gov/portal/site/uscis/menuitem.5af9bb95919f35e66f 614176543f6d1a/?vgnextchannel=b328194d3e88d010VgnVCM100000 48f3d6a1RCRD&vgnextoid=04a295c4f635f010VgnVCM1000000ecd190a RCRD.

enforced. We had, in a relatively short time, decided to change our policy and "control" our borders. Push/pull, come/go, go/come continued, but then when migrants got here, it was no-no. People were forced to cross through the desert areas of Agua Prieta/Douglas, Arizona in the late 1990s and early 2000s, but by the mid- and late-2000s the flow of migration was pushed to even more remote and deadly areas like the deserts and mountains east of Yuma and the Altar Valley southwest of Tucson. Has the strategy been effective? Despite our attempts to "control" the border, the presence of undocumented immigrants has continued to grow, due to the push/pull factors, throughout virtually the entire country.

In 1994, I was teaching Spanish in Clover, South Carolina; other than myself and one other nonnative Spanish-speaking teacher, there were no other Spanish-speaking persons in town. I went back there ten years later, in 2004. Ten years after we started beefing up our border "control" programs and implementing Operation Gatekeeper, there was a large banner decorated with Mexican and Guatemalan flags hanging from the roof of the Piggly Wiggly grocery store with the words: "Tenemos productos hispanos"—we have Hispanic products. The First Baptist Church was offering free English as a Second Language classes. At the bank, a sign asked if you wanted service in English or Spanish. In ten years, Clover, South Carolina, had gone from having two non-native Spanish-speaking people to having a sizeable enough population that grocery stores and banks were marketing to them and churches were reaching out to them.

And this anecdote could be repeated in many towns, sub-urbs, and cities throughout the United States, precisely at a time when our government decided to get serious about enforcing the border. In 1994, there were 4.5 million undoc-umented persons in the United States. Now, after spending billions of dollars to "seal" the border, there are more than 11 million—the number had increased to over 12 million prior to the recession that began in 2008. There have been other more serious and even deadly consequences to our decision to pursue a border enforcement strategy that used the deserts and mountains as lethal deterrents without considering the power of the economic and family push and pull factors.

Increased Death

Since the inception of Operation Gatekeeper in 1994, three times more people have died in the deserts of the southwest while seeking to reach the "American Dream" than the number of persons who died in the attacks of 9/11. More people have died crossing the U.S./Mexico border trying to provide a livelihood for their families than the combined number of U.S. soldiers who have died in the Iraq and Afghanistan wars. Since 1994, over 5,500 bodies have been found. That doesn't include the deaths of persons whose bodies have never been found.

Boon to the Smuggling Industry

An irony of our increased border enforcement is that it has been accompanied by an increase in the size, sophistication, and wealth of smuggling operations on both sides of the border. Smuggling of drugs and people is a growth industry. In its working paper "An Analysis of Migrant Smuggling Costs along the Southwest Border," the Department of Homeland Security provides data tracking the increased costs of smuggling with the increase of border enforcement.[8] The data presented in the DHS paper corresponds closely with the information of the local residents in Agua Prieta with whom I have talked over the years. According to them, the cost to get across the border has risen from $50 to $100 prior to 1994, if a smuggler was needed at all, to $800 in

---

8 http://www.dhs.gov/xlibrary/assets/statistics/publications/ois-smuggling-wp.pdf.

1998 when I first arrived on the border, to $2,000 or more today—with a much higher risk of being caught, injured, or killed. The DHS's working paper states that the increased costs for smuggling are only a "potential deterrent."

Increased Injury

Seventeen years of using the deserts and mountains as lethal deterrents and the increasing height of fencing during those years have resulted in a significant increase in the number of persons sustaining traumatic physical injuries while crossing the border. In addition to the intense suffering experienced by the migrants who have not been deterred by our policies that intentionally increase the risk for their crossing, border hospitals have experienced financial and emotional stress as they receive more patients with broken bones or severe complications from hypothermia and hyperthermia. The increasing number of life-threatening and life-altering injuries also has a psychological impact on our agents who are tasked with securing our borders, as they are often the first responders to migrants with compound fractures, severe dehydration, and other painful physical conditions.

Entry of States into the Realm of Writing Immigration Legislation

Despite the federal government's massive attempts to "stop the flow of migration," communities throughout the United States, many like Clover, South Carolina, that had not previously been destinations for migrants from south of the border, saw a swell of newcomers to their communities, especially during the years in which the economy in the United States was growing. As economic and cultural fears in communities increased, many anti-immigrant groups began organizing, putting political pressure on local and state governments to do something about the "immigration problem." The argument was often that the states needed to do something since the federal government was not "doing anything." As we have seen, the federal government had been doing something in a big way—it was just ineffective and less powerful than the economic and familial factors driving immigration.

In 2010, Arizona passed SB 1070, at the time the toughest antiauthorized immigrant law in the United States. Despite being challenged constitutionally and having an injunction placed on it, the law became a marker that many other states tried to match or surpass. Since the passage of SB 1070, South Carolina, Georgia, and Utah have passed similar laws. On June 9, 2011, Governor Robert Bentley of Alabama signed HB 56 into law, which surpassed Arizona's SB 1070 as the toughest law in the land.

On June 25, 2012, the U.S. Supreme Court ruled that multiple provisions of SB 1070 are unconstitutional. The Court did uphold the section that allows police to request proof of immigration status. The ruling judged that the states were not preempting federal authority by requesting identification. The Obama administration promptly announced that it would only respond to local law enforcement's immigration requests on the basis of its priorities of focusing on persons who have committed felonies or have previous deportations and would not send immigration officers to take persons into custody who were stopped on traffic violations. In addition, civil rights groups are suing to stop the "papers, please" statute as a violation of a person's civil rights.

Conclusion and Challenge

My colleague Jesus Gallegos and I were speaking to a men's breakfast and prayer group in Loveland, Colorado, and were sharing some of the difficulties of people's lives on the border. Toward the end of our presentation, one brother raised his hand and challenged us: "It's well and good to talk about how bad things are, but you need to do something about it." His challenge to us is rooted in the call of Jesus Christ who, faced with the news of the imprisonment of John, begins his ministry proclaiming and living out the good news of the kingdom of God.

We've rehearsed a bit of how "bad things are" and reviewed the complexity of immigration issues confronting our nations. The rest of the book will share visions of how the church is called to respond in faith to the challenges and opportunities of immigration. In the face of death, we are called to witness to life, to unity in the face of division, to hope in the face of fear, to love in the face of hate because we are the body of Christ. Listen to the words of Jesus:

"The time has come. The kingdom of God is near. Repent and trust the good news!"

—Mark Adams
Presbyterian Church (USA) mission co-worker
Frontera de Cristo (www.fronteradecristo.org)
Lent 2013

1 | Immigration

A Bishop's Perspective

Minerva G. Carcaño

Every summer since becoming a bishop I have taken a road trip from my home in Scottsdale, Arizona, to my birthplace in South Texas. The 1,100 miles between Scottsdale and Edinburg, Texas, give me much time to ponder life and ministry. I always take the route closest to the border between the United States and Mexico. Family and friends encourage me to take the route through El Paso and then on through San Antonio, Texas, but the border always beckons to me. As I travel through Arizona, then across New Mexico, and then finally down the long stretch of Texas that leads me home, I remember.

I have spent most of my life and ministry on this border. It has shaped and nurtured me as well as given me a lens through which I see life. I am the daughter of a father who

1

came to the United States under the Bracero Program, a labor agreement between the United States and Mexico that allowed men to come and work in the United States. As a *bracero*, a term referring to the arms he provided the U.S. economy, my father labored in the cotton and vegetable fields of South Texas. It was there that he met my mother, the daughter of a Mexican immigrant mother and a father born and reared in Texas.

Born into this border family, I have always known myself as a daughter of the border; that place that joins people, cultures, and languages in a way that makes one a citizen of one country with roots deep enough to also tap the springs of life of the country just beyond. Such roots do not easily allow one to side with the prejudices of one or the other country, for to do so is to violate a part of one's own personhood. Such an identity comes with its own vulnerability. The vulnerability of being a daughter of the border was put on full display on the very first few days of my episcopacy.

Assigned to an episcopal area that covers most of Arizona, southern Nevada, and the California communities that rest on the western edge of the Colorado River, I came to the Phoenix Episcopal Area of The United Methodist Church on September 1, 2004. At that moment the Arizona state legislature was considering Arizona Proposition 200, causing much heated debate. One of the first things requested of me as I assumed my responsibilities as a bishop was to write what would become my regular monthly epistles to the faithful. A great believer in ministry that is contextual and socially relevant, I decided to comment on Arizona Proposition 200. Besides, I thought, it would give me an opportunity to share a bit about myself.

I shared with my new constituency that being faced by Arizona Proposition 200 had taken me back to the days of my childhood when, as the daughter of an immigrant, I would sit with my father at our kitchen table and hear with troubled heart the stories of how he had come to this country. My father had come across the U.S./Mexico border as a strong young man to work in the agricultural fields of the Rio Grande Valley of South Texas, fields that have fed this country through times of war and peace. He was one of thousands of Mexican laborers who have toiled on that land for the sake of U.S. families, his own family benefiting along the way as well. He worked long, hard days until the day he was told that his labor was no longer needed; the Bracero Program was over for him. Returning to his village in the mountains of north-central Mexico, he found a community whose own agricultural economy had been devastated through the absence of their young men who had gone north. Soon he found himself with no options but to return to Texas. The preference of his heart would have been to remain in his beloved community and country.

When my father attempted to return to Texas, he was told that there was no longer room for him; it mattered not that he had given long hard years of service to this country. Yes, he had been compensated for his work but at the bottom of the pay scale, with no labor rights to speak of, and often cheated by corrupt middle men. Far from home and with no resources, my father joined the many others who yearly, to this day, swim across the Rio Grande River in search of sustenance and hope. It was not an easy journey. On one occasion he had been pulled out of the waters of the great river by U.S. border officials, accused of transporting drugs, and threatened with death.

At that point in his life, my father did not even know what constituted a drug and had with him only a change of clothes in a plastic bag and a few pesos in his pocket. He remembered how the border officials had placed him in an interrogation room with glaring lights and told him he would not leave that room alive if he didn't confess that he was involved in smuggling drugs or told them who he worked for. My father had no dealings with the drug world. He simply wanted to provide food and care for his family in Mexico. Weary, and convinced that his life would end in that place, he told the border officials that they would have to just kill him because he had nothing to confess. A day later, exhausted from the terrifying experience, he was released and sent back to Mexico. My father would never again fully trust the U.S. legal system even after becoming a U.S. citizen.

In spite of his ordeal at the border, my father continued to cross into this country. It was not an act of defiance, but the simple human struggle for survival. Eventually, through marriage, he was able to become a U.S. citizen. I was in the third grade when my father prepared for and took his U.S. citizenship test. I helped him study for the test and no one was prouder of my father when he became a U.S. citizen than I. My father's story is the story of men and women, children and young people who today risk their lives as they cross the border. I would venture to say that the majority of them would prefer to remain in their native land but come to this country out of great human need and despair.

It was against this backdrop of life that I read Proposition 200, the Arizona Taxpayer and Citizen Protection Act. My research and study of its components led me to determine that it was a costly proposition not only in taxpayer dollars, but in the potentially negative impact it could have on communities across the state. From the perspective of Christian faith, Proposition 200 would create unjust law. I do not oppose immigration laws per se. Immigration laws are necessary for civil society to organize its life and care for its people, but immigration laws must be just and fair. Proposition 200, however, did nothing to help achieve such a level of law. It did nothing to address true immigration concerns, but it did carry the potential of undermining the civil liberties and human rights of persons and further aggravating the hostility that already existed between documented and undocumented persons in the state of Arizona.

I encouraged United Methodists to consider the God whom we serve, a God who loves the immigrant and calls us to love the immigrant as well. I shared that I would be opposing Proposition 200 and invited others to prayerfully discern for themselves how they would respond to the proposition. I encouraged all to be responsible citizens and to vote. Sending forth my very first episcopal word to the people I was called to serve and lead, I wondered how it would be received. The response was quick and direct. It came in the form of an e-mail that contained but one sentence:

> I respectfully request that the bishop confine her epistles to matters of the church and stay out of politics.

When I read the respondent's words, the first thought that went through my mind was "What Bible is this person reading, for it is not the Bible I am reading!" The person suggested that I confine my words and work to matters of the church, but what would Jesus define as matters of the church? The Bible I read states that Jesus calls us to welcome the stranger, says it is the righteous thing to do and, even more, that our salvation is dependent on our doing so (Matthew 25:31–46). The Jesus I came to know in Holy Scripture calls us to love our neighbor as we love ourselves and never distinguishes between the native born and the immigrant neighbor. If anything, Jesus calls us to favor the one who suffers most. Jesus calls us to be servants to others rather than to sit at table expecting to be served; to be last rather than first (Mark 9:33–37). This Jesus reminds us that we are the people of God who have and will always be immigrants in this world, for we are citizens of the reign of God, and who, because we are God's own and know what it means to be an immigrant, do not ever oppress the immigrant, rather welcome the immigrant as one of our own.

As Christians we are in fact called to love the immigrant (Leviticus 19:33).

As I prayerfully study Holy Scripture, I find clear evidence that Jesus took on the political empire of his time in all its brokenness and evil, holding up the alternative vision of communities of justice and peace where every single person is known to be of sacred worth in the eyes of God. Communities patterned after Jesus's own hope are communities where the orphan, the widow, the sojourner, the poor, and the outcast are cared for with a preferential love. Jesus proclaims that the reign of God has arrived with the fullness of God's own redemption, justice, and peace; a reign that shall have the last word.

So what are matters of the church? According to the witness of Holy Scripture, all of life falls under the care and concern of Christ Jesus, and thus as Christ's disciples, we believe that all of life with its personal and social, its political, socioeconomic, and cultural dimensions falls under the concern of the church. Jesus passionately cares about all of life, and about each one of us. What I came to know through this initial experience of speaking on the issue of immigration was that many of our church members had very little awareness of what scripture says about how we are to treat the immigrant, and even worse, that regardless of what scripture says, there was no strong desire to follow what scripture teaches us about receiving and loving the immigrant.

A year later, I was challenged by the Board of Church and Society of our area to lead a walk in the desert of Arizona. These leaders believed that getting out into the desert and learning firsthand about immigration across the border that Arizona shares with the Mexican state of Sonora would help us better understand the situation. I agreed to lead such a walk and extended an invitation to all who wanted to join us. Over one hundred people joined the walk in the desert: conservatives, liberals, moderates, and the undecided! As

I walked up the middle aisle of the church where we gathered for our orientation for this desert walk, I could hear the comments. For the most part they were political comments. Few were the comments about Christian faith and what faith required of us in such a situation. For some, that would change as we experienced the desert and encountered immigrants. The images from that walk in the desert are many, but the two that haunt me to this day are about young people.

We were guided out into the desert by leaders of the Humane Borders project, which extends humanitarian assistance to immigrants by providing water stations on the routes that immigrants use as they move from the south to the north. As our time in the desert was ending, our Humane Borders guides told me that there was one more spot they wanted us to see but only a handful of persons could go because the spot was on government protected land and we had only received permission for a few to travel there. I was given the opportunity to select a few persons to travel with me further into the desert. I tried to select persons of varying perspectives on the issue of immigration. We went into the desert together as others began the journey back to Tucson, Arizona, where we would gather and reflect on what we had experienced.

There in a remote section of the desert stood a tree that had become a sanctuary of faith. A cross made of mesquite wood leaned against the tree. Rosaries swung from the branches of the tree. Small mesquite bark crosses marked spots where water bottles and coins had been carefully left. I saw a small bible and a dusty note that encouraged immigrants to trust in God as they journeyed. I looked around, searching for signs of the individuals who had created this holy place, but saw nothing to inform me. I wondered when they had been there and what had led them to this place. As I looked up, our guide gently smiled at me, recognizing the confusion I was feeling and invited those of us at the tree to gather so that he could explain what we were seeing.

A young immigrant woman in her early twenties had died beneath that tree. Dehydration and the heat of the desert had consumed her. For some time, Humane Borders had been attempting to convince the U.S. Bureau of Land Management to grant them permission to place a water tank for immigrants crossing the desert through this remote area, but to no avail. The death of this young woman, however, had become the persuasive force and finally a water station had been allowed. Our guide pointed just beyond the tree where we could see a slender long metal pole with a blue flag at the top, a sign that at that spot was a water station for the weary and the thirsty to stop and rest and quench their thirst. The story of the death of this young woman that had brought water to this place became known and had led immigrants to memorialize her by marking the spot where she had died. Because of the sacrifice of her life, others would live. But why does anyone have to die in the desert in search of life?

The other walkers had left the desert ahead of us, but we soon caught up with them at First United Methodist Church in Tucson. We had just arrived when a woman came running to me, crying and in a state of obvious despair, to tell me about the boys she and those traveling with her had seen. She had been sitting in the back row of the van looking out the window and reflecting on all she had seen and experienced in the desert when suddenly she saw what seemed at first sight to be a body lying underneath a bush. She screamed for the van driver to stop because someone was possibly hurt or even dead in the desert. When the van stopped, everyone got out and moved toward the bush, and lo and behold under the bush they found two young boys. Assuring them they would not hurt them, the boys came out from under the bush. They were no more than fourteen years old and yet there they were in the middle of the desert all alone, hiding under a bush. When asked what they were doing in the desert, they readily shared their story.

They were immigrants seeking a way to help sustain themselves and their families back home. They had come all the way to this place in the desert with a group of more than twenty persons but when the *coyote* (the term used on the border for human smugglers) had come for them as planned, he did not have enough room in his vehicle for all of them, so these two boys had been left behind. They were the expendable ones, alone without any adult to stand up for them and defend them, alone in a country they did not know, alone without food or water. We had carried brown paper sacks filled with nonperishable foods and water bottles into the desert, so this small contingency of our group gave those boys food and water and words of encouragement. They could do no more than that for fear of breaking U.S. laws. The woman who had first caught sight of them was beside herself. What would those boys do alone in the desert? Would they be able to survive? Where would they go? They had told them that the best thing was for them to turn themselves in to the Border Patrol, but they had looked at each other and then the taller of the two had said that they were headed for San Francisco, California. Could they tell them which way to go?

Some time later, I was invited to preach at a church in my area on a Sunday when the church was focusing on children and the church's sacred responsibility to care for children. I found it quite easy to speak about caring for all God's children, mentioning the different places in life where the children of our area found themselves. I spoke of caring for children of all races and cultures, of all socioeconomic status, and of all faith perspectives. In passing, I mentioned caring for immigrant children who suffer in the desert of our southern border, the emphasis being on caring for all God's children in our midst. The reference to immigrant children was the briefest of statements. This brief statement had come as a sharing of what others had seen of children in the desert and my having seen children's pajamas, pretty little dresses, tiny toothbrushes, and even a child's stroller: all things that had been found in the desert where immigrants cross over into this country. Well, you would have thought that instead of speaking a gospel truth I had blasphemed, for the very next day I was pulled into an e-mail exchange with a member of that church who challenged me.

Early Monday morning I was confronted by an e-mail from a woman who had heard me. It was a sharp challenge. The challenge was not so much what I had said about the care of children, but rather that I had dared to say that there were immigrant children in the desert! I tried explaining that while I personally had not seen these immigrant children, others had, and in the desert they had found things that obviously belonged to children. The outcome of our back-and-forth e-mails was that this church member finally directly accused me of lying. There were no immigrant children in the desert, she insisted. Eventually I let go of the encounter, but could not shake off the slur of being called a liar. At some point, I began to question whether there truly were immigrant children in the desert. Others had seen them and collected their left-behind belongings, but I could not say that I was a firsthand witness to such a fact. The following summer, however, I personally met the children in the desert.

On a renewal leave, I decided to spend time in service to immigrants. I did so because I have consistently found that my faith is renewed by being in the presence of immigrants who have no doubt of God's existence and loving care for humanity and all of creation. I went to our southern border with a coordinator for mission volunteers and spent five days caring for immigrants. On several of these days, we walked and worked with persons who have committed their lives to extending care to immigrants in the desert. It is not an uncommon experience for immigrants to find themselves stranded in the desert either because they have been injured on the arduous immigrant journey or by being separated from the group with whom they were traveling. Sometimes they travel alone, running out of water and food and becoming too weak to continue. At that time, three hundred immigrants were dying every year in Arizona's border desert.

We did not find any immigrants on that desert visit, but we did see their fresh footprints, their abandoned campsites, their empty water bottles, and their backpacks. Early one morning we saw what appeared to be a group of immigrants, but by the time we arrived at the spot where we had seen them at a distance, they were gone. More experienced volunteers tell us that immigrants have learned how to disappear into the desert in order to survive. We called out to them that we were friends, *Samaritanos*—Samaritans seeking only to help them. We left them food and water at the spot where we had seen them.

One day we found a bright orange Church World Service blanket in a small clearing amidst a circle of mesquite trees and we felt such joy and some definite pride that our ecumenical efforts had given protection to our immigrant brothers and sisters in that place. On that same day I saw for myself a sign of the children in the desert. We came upon a large cluster of bushes and saw the typical trash left behind by immigrants: water bottles, backpacks, and tin cans once containing precious food. But there was more at this particular place: women's clothing, a dried-out bottle of women's hand cream and a small perfume bottle, and then as I moved a rock with my foot, I saw it. It was a baby bottle right there on the desert floor. I suddenly felt a surge of deep sorrow in my spirit as I realized that a suckling baby had been in the desert, exposed to hot days and cold nights, rattlesnakes and scorpions, possibly the lack of food and water, feeling the fullness of the anguish, anxiety, and fear of whoever was carrying that baby. I kept that baby bottle as a reminder of the horrors of the immigrant journey, and as a sure sign that there are children in the desert and we must care for them. I began to feel more assured of what I had been preaching and saying. Then, almost as if to banish any remaining doubt, the next day I actually saw them.

Their names were Jocelyn and Melvin, ten and eight years of age, older sister and younger brother. We had gone to Nogales, Sonora, Mexico, to serve immigrants who are deported back to Mexico. Busloads of immigrants are dumped on the U.S./Mexico border several times a day at this place, among others. We joined a team of U.S. and Mexican volunteers who receive these immigrants on the Mexican side of the border, providing them with a cup of Ramen soup, a change of clothing, and a bit of orientation. Our immigrant brothers and sisters are tired, dirty, disoriented, and always broke and broken. It was there that we washed the feet of the immigrants, cutting away the most horrible and enormous black-and-blue foot blisters I have ever seen, nursing their feet with antibiotic creams, then bandaging them as carefully as we could so we did not add to their already unbearable pain. It was the last bus of the afternoon that blessed my life with Jocelyn and Melvin.

When we saw that bus arrive, we went out to meet those being deported, welcoming them and offering them respite. After all had apparently gotten off the bus and we started to walk with the deported immigrants back to a simple tent set up for their care, someone pointed out that there was yet another immigrant. He got off the bus carefully and began to walk toward us. He was limping terribly, holding on to his left leg. We thought he might have sprained or even broken his leg, but as two of us met him and asked whether he was alright, he informed us that he was tired and weary, but was alright. He had a disability from birth that made him limp.

Once we knew what his condition was, we were able to see beyond him and realize that he was not alone. Walking right behind him holding on to his shirt were Jocelyn and Melvin, his children. They were a family from Chiapas, Mexico. This young man's wife, Jocelyn and Melvin's mother, was suffering from very serious gallbladder disease and could not travel, but he had no work, and they had no food and no other means to sustain themselves. They had made the difficult decision to leave home and attempt to reach the United States, in order to provide for their needs and care for that wife and mother all the way back in Chiapas.

As I washed that father's dusty and blistered feet, he told me their immigrant story. He was a corn farmer left destitute by the impact of the North American Free Trade Agreement. I was focusing on caring for his battered feet when a silence came over us. I looked up and saw that tears had begun to fall upon his checks. As I looked at him, working hard to hold back my own tears provoked by his deep sadness, he told me how on their fourth day in the desert he had become convinced that he would lose his little boy. Melvin had become dehydrated and fainted on the desert floor. Jocelyn and Melvin were leaning on their father's shoulders, one on each side, watching and listening to their own life story. I gulped back my emotions, and turning to Melvin, said to him, "You are a very brave boy." Melvin didn't lose a beat. Looking adoringly at his sister across his father's shoulders, he responded, "I'm not as brave as my sister. She never fainted." Jocelyn blushed and looked away. It was a tender moment of fraternal love, the bond between Melvin and Jocelyn having been made that much stronger by the experience of human struggle for survival that no child should every have to face.

When we left the care tent and said good-bye to Jocelyn, Melvin, and their father, my companion and I gave that father all the money we had, which was not much. They were not the only immigrants left at that care station, but we felt that with two young children he was the most in need of help. Silence fell over the small group of immigrants that was still there when we gave the father that money. I sensed that they were holding their breath, expecting that we might consider giving them some financial help as well. As we left, I looked straight ahead, not able to face the other immigrants, for I could not help them in the same way. It was a painful moment for us, but suddenly the heaviness of the moment was penetrated and transformed into unexpected joy as we heard those immigrant men and women say, "Gracias, hermano (Thank you, brother)!" And out of the corner of my eye I saw Jocelyn and Melvin's father turning and sharing what little we had given him with the other immigrants. What a witness to those children, to Jocelyn and Melvin, and what a witness to us. It was the sound and the sight of the reign of God!

Yes, unfortunately there are immigrant children walking and suffering in the desert places of this country, but God is with them, and we should be with them as well.

That precious time with Melvin and Jocelyn reminded me of Jesus's words: "Allow the children to come to me. Don't forbid them, because God's kingdom belongs to people like these children. . . . Then he hugged the children and blessed them" (Mark 10:14b, 16, CEB). I looked for the time and place of this passage to put it in context, but found none. I believe there is no time or place mentioned in relation to this passage of scripture because it is a passage for all times and all places. In every moment and in every place we are to care for the children, taking them into our arms and blessing them with the very love of Christ Jesus.

Our care for the children of this world will help form their hearts and their character and, through them, the culture of the world all around us will be determined. I believe Jesus was hoping we would see that our care for children holds the greatest opportunity to usher in the reign of God. How will we care for the children of this world, the children in our families and in our neighborhoods, our towns and cities, and in our congregations? How will we help form them, nurture and teach them to be children of God's mercy, justice, and peace?

Shortly after I met Jocelyn and Melvin and their father, I happened to be with another child. We were listening together to presidential candidates on the radio. At one of the breaks, that child said with great conviction, "If I could vote I wouldn't vote for anybody who gives my money away to people I don't even know!" That child was nine years old, and someone had taught her that attitude; an attitude of self-centeredness, of greed, of lack of love for neighbor; an attitude that ignores the fact that we are all children of God and therefore brothers and sisters to each other!

If our children see us ignoring the plight of the immigrant child, what do we teach them? Do we not teach them that immigrant children are worthless, not worth our attention or care? And what do we teach the immigrant children if they never see anyone extend a caring hand to them? Do we not confirm that lesson of worthlessness and do we not teach them that the world is cruel and unjust? Will either lesson bring them or us any justice, any peace, any joy?

While Jesus welcomed the children, the disciples chastised them and attempted to turn them away (Mark 10:13b). Have we considered the fact that those children who gathered around Jesus were taking it all in? Jesus blesses the children and all of us when he does not allow stern words of chastisement and rejection to be the lasting experience of the children who sought his blessing. Jesus became indignant—showing those children who were present and all who have over the generations heard what happened that day with the children that they are to be cared for, that they are important in God's reign. In children's weakness, in their vulnerability, in their dependency on others, is found our opportunity to shape the world around us and to help bring in even the reign of God! We must be the strongest voice for justice and God's reign that we can muster; a voice for the children. I regret that we were not a stronger voice for justice or a more faithful witness to young people when the state of Arizona faced its Senate Bill 1070.

Presented as a bill that would do what the federal government had failed to do, namely stop undocumented immigration into the state of Arizona as well as rid the state of as many undocumented immigrants as possible, SB 1070 (signed into law on April 23, 2010) did nothing good for the communities of the state of Arizona. Instead, it led the state into a number of lawsuits around the constitutionality of such a law, and further aggravated an economic recession in the state as civil rights groups and powerful businesses boycotted the state because of what they determined was a blatantly racist law. Immigrants, documented and undocumented, left the state out of concern for the safety of their families, taking with them their economic contributions as well. Fear and division arose in local communities. Some communities experienced an increase in racial profiling. Communities of faith serving immigrant families lost members as these immigrant families also chose to leave the state rather than live in a place with an anti-immigrant spirit, and one now supported by law. An immigrant mother, and a leader in one of our United Methodist congregations, said to us as she informed us of her family's decision to leave the state of Arizona, "We cannot have our children growing up in a state where they are hated."

The Friday Arizona governor Jan Brewer signed SB 1070 into law was a day of deep sadness for many of us. I believe it was a day of shame for Arizona and for the country that will be remembered in our history for generations to come. I further believe that the signing of SB 1070 into law was an action of political expediency rather than political courage. Signed into law in an election year, we would later see that such an action had garnered votes for those who supported SB 1070. It was nevertheless an unwise, shortsighted, and mean-spirited piece of legislation. Contrary to Governor Brewer's public statements in support of SB 1070, it was not what was best for Arizona.

At the very moment that Governor Brewer signed SB 1070 into law, a group of us religious leaders were at the Arizona State Capitol providing pastoral support for 1,500 young people who were gathered there, devastated when Governor Brewer signed into law this clearly anti-immigrant bill. Those young people ranged from middle school to college age. They had held a vigil of prayer and presence at the Arizona State Capitol grounds since the day SB 1070 had been introduced. They had launched a Twitter and e-mail campaign that had grown their numbers in a matter of days from a dozen to the 1,500 gathered at the State Capitol that afternoon. When it had become known that this was the day that the governor would make her decision about this potentially life-threatening bill that would affect them and their families, these young people had left their classrooms and come to the capitol, hundreds of them walking great distances to give their witness for fairness and justice.

The signing of SB 1070 by Governor Brewer caused great fear in the hearts of the young people gathered at the Arizona State Capitol and in the hearts of many others living across the state. They feared they would be stopped on the streets of the communities where they lived, and at the places where they studied and worked, just because of the color of their skin and the sound of their voice. Many of them feared that their immigrant parents would be deported and that their families would be separated and trampled by a rampant hatred that was out of control in Arizona. But it was even more than that. In their youthful idealism, these young people had dared to believe that our Arizona governor would do the right thing.

As people of faith in Arizona and across this country, we cannot allow the further destruction of the hope and conviction of these young persons and their families, our brothers and sisters; that hope and conviction that justice will prevail in every unjust life situation. Across the United States, young people like those who gathered at the Arizona State Capitol on that April afternoon continue to hold up the vision and the hope of justice, God's own justice, even as we fail them. Their spirit inspires my heart.

As the afternoon sun began to fall on the Arizona State Capitol as Governor Brewer signed SB 1070 into law, my own spirit was lifted up as I was invited to the platform to address these young people. I made my best effort to encourage them and to affirm for them that we religious leaders would not abandon them. I encouraged them to dig deep into the reservoirs of their own faith and to continue to be faithful and courageous witnesses. As I finished my words, the young man who was leading this young people's rally took my hand and asked me to lead them in prayer. Leaning close to me he said, "Bishop, lead us in the Lord's Prayer. We all know that prayer." And then looking at me with an obvious question in his mind, he whispered in my ear, "Bishop, can you kneel? We need to kneel for this prayer." I smiled at him and said, "Yes, I can still kneel." Holding hands, we knelt, 1,500 young people kneeling with us on the grounds of the Arizona State Capitol. Together we prayed the Lord's Prayer. As we finished praying, a hush came over us, a gentle breeze blew upon us, tears were wiped away, and I saw courage return to the faces of those young people. At that moment I knew two things with deep certainty. I knew that these young people would lead us even in ways that we had not begun to imagine. I also knew in the sacredness of that moment that God was with us; God who forgets not His own.

The U.S. immigration landscape is treacherous today, affecting our state and national politics, economics, the sociocultural development of our towns and cities, and our communities of faith. No one experiences how treacherous it is more than immigrants themselves. The stories I tell are the immigrant's own stories as I continue to encounter them in life and ministry. One day I met an immigrant father who had been detained at his work in North Carolina. For a decade he had been working as a pipe installer for a family-owned company. He had been detained in North Carolina for a time, then moved to Arizona and from there deported back to Mexico. His experience is reflective of an Immigration and Customs Enforcement (ICE) strategy that moves detained immigrants to areas for deportation from which it will be difficult for them to return to those places where they were living when they were detained.

This man left behind an eight-year-old son. When we asked him what had happened to his son, he told us that his Anglo, U.S. citizen boss in North Carolina had gone and found his son for him and taken him to his home. Since being detained, he had been able to make contact with his boss only twice. Both times his boss had told him to find a way to get back to North Carolina because he needed his good labor, and his son missed him. When I met him, it had been three months since he had last seen his son.

Soon after the passage of SB 1070 I came across a young man sitting at a bus station in Nogales, Sonora, Mexico. He was fully bilingual, fluent in English and Spanish, but that was of little help to him. He looked worn, worried, and disoriented. When I asked him what had happened to him, he told me that he had been at a gas station in Mesa, Arizona, when a policeman came over to him and asked him for identification. He didn't have any, though he has lived in the United States all of his life. He was in Mexico because the encounter with the police officer at the gas station had led to his deportation. He told us he knew no one in Mexico. His family all lived in Arizona. He did not know what he was going to do. A pastor who was with me took down his name and address and promised to contact his family. His family did not know where he was.

Later that same day, I found myself in the middle of a dozen children huddled in a room of a Mexican detention center for immigrant children. On that particular day the children ranged from ages eleven to seventeen, though I was told that on other days, toddlers could be found among them. Their parents are living and working in the United States. Their families were trying to reunite them with their parents, but these children had been caught by the U.S. Border Patrol while on their immigrant journey and deported back to Mexico. A relative must now make the trip to this particular place in northern Mexico, bringing official documentation to prove a blood relationship in order for these children to be released to them. Some of their families live thousands of miles away and may have already spent all the resources they had to get these children to the United States. Many will have no means to travel to this place. These children know the circumstances of their families, even the youngest among them, and fear that they will never be reunited with their families.

I have come to know a good number of immigrant women who survive by cleaning other people's homes. The story of one who has become a friend is a typical story among immigrants. The woman of the house pays her in cash because this cleaning woman is undocumented and the woman of the house knows the trouble she would be in if she were caught employing an undocumented person. She also knows that she would have to pay her more if she followed the law. This cleaning woman has three daughters, two of them born in the United States. Her husband works in landscaping for an established firm. He, too, is undocumented, but he has a social security number, the benefits of which he will never see. He says, "For now, it is enough that I get paid today."

Husband and wife work every day of the week except Sunday. They want their children to honor and respect the Sabbath. They are members of a Lutheran congregation.

They barely make it week by week, but somehow they find a way to financially sustain an elderly aunt back home. This friend who cleans houses, rears children, cares for others, and is committed to Christ Jesus, tells me that she and her family live each day fearful that the U.S. authorities will find out that they are living in this country without documentation, but she quickly adds that whatever happens, she knows that God will be with them. I sit with her, her precious, beautiful daughters playing close by, and I wonder what will happen to them. I especially worry about her oldest daughter, who has lived most of her life in the United States but was born in Mexico.

That oldest daughter represents young people all over the United States who were brought to this country as children, undocumented under U.S. immigration laws. They are young people who know the United States as home, with a good number of them knowing no other country. Some are fully bilingual and bicultural, while others have assimilated to the degree that the only language they speak is English, their identity fully grounded in the culture and ways of life of the United States. These young people had no choice in the matter. Many of them have grown up in homes where it was impossible to rectify their immigration status. In many ways, they are trapped.

As they complete their public education and consider a college degree, these young people find that there is no financial help to assist them because of their immigration status. In most states they will be required to pay out-of-state tuition to attend college, an economic hardship of enormous proportions for immigrant young people and their families. Those who are able to somehow make it through college will find that internships in their field of study will exclude them because they are undocumented. They also face the fact that even with a college degree, U.S. immigration laws will prohibit them from working in the United States.

For over a decade legislative efforts have been made to grant undocumented immigrant young people the opportunity of higher education and a pathway to citizenship through study or military service. The most recent failed DREAM Act is one such legislative effort. Unfortunately, not even this most basic legislation to assist immigrant children has been able to gather sufficient support for passage. I believe that at the root of this cruel attitude toward immigrant children and young people we will find racism and nativism.

One morning I came back to my office after a short vacation to a pile of form letters from the United Methodist chapter of an organization that claims to alone know what God expects of the church and is out to make sure United Methodists and other mainline Protestants shape up or ship out. The pile of form letters was a bit of a "welcome back from vacation" gift! There were over one hundred copies of the same message. The only original thing, from form letter to form letter, was the name and address in the fill-in-the-blank section and an occasional creative curse on the side. The message was that I and all United Methodist bishops should quit ministering to immigrants unless, of course, they were definitely Christians.

How these persons measure the validity of another's faith is beyond me, but what was crystal clear is that being brown and coming from the South did not measure up. But forget about their woefully lacking understanding of faith. What I want to know is where these brothers and sisters get their understanding of what it means to be faithful? I had a conversation through correspondence that stretched over a couple of years with a member of one of the churches in my area who appears to resonate with these Christians; that conversation helped me understand their thinking.

Over a period of time this church member and I went back and forth. It began with a letter of concern from him. Did I not know that every time I spoke about the immigration situation, whether in a public statement or in my preaching and teaching, I was advocating the breaking of the law? I shared with him my understanding of what scripture teaches us about how we are to treat the immigrant, and I sent him copies of our denomination's statements about immigration. He was quick to inform me that I did not speak for him and that he was sure that other bishops of our church surely did not believe as I did. I then sent him copies of the statements of our United Methodist Council of Bishops that call all United Methodists to treat immigrants with the compassion of Christ's own heart.

Back and forth we went in our conversation, a conversation that not only failed to change either of our minds, but that always left me feeling that we were not fully communicating with each other and that there was something I was missing. Finally, he sent me his last letter and what I was missing was revealed to me. In the last paragraph of his lengthy but eloquent letter he said to me, "I long for the day when my church will realize that the most important task it has is to defend U.S. democracy." It was suddenly abundantly clear to me.

We had been on different pages all along. We did not have the same understanding of the identity and purpose of the church. I find neither in scripture nor in church teaching, in reason or in experience, a way to justify an understanding of the church as an agent of a human political order. Our task as Christians is not to defend U.S. democracy or any other form of government. As Christians, our task is to share the good news we have known in Jesus Christ and to follow in Jesus's footsteps, living as he did. I understand my task as a bishop of the church as that of helping Christians under my spiritual care to know and remember who we are. As Christians we are the people of the reign of God; yes, citizens of man-made political states, respectful of human laws, but above all, citizens of the reign of God called to be faithful to the One who alone is Sovereign; faithful to the One who calls us to welcome and love the immigrant.

In Matthew 25:31–46, Jesus speaks of what is expected of us as members of the reign of God. It is a rich passage, full of faithful guidance for how we are to live our lives as Christians, and includes a clear reference to the immigrant. Jesus directly tells us that when we welcome the stranger, we welcome him, and when we fail to welcome the stranger, we fail to welcome him. Jesus is abundantly clear. Our salvation is inextricably linked to how we treat the immigrant. Granted, for many reasons, welcoming the stranger is not an easy thing.

Is the immigrant we welcome trustworthy? Will caring for the immigrant eat up resources we need for caring for our own? Why should we have to assume the care of immigrants; should we not expect the countries they come from to care for their own?

Welcoming the stranger as Jesus asks us to do is difficult for us, particularly in our U.S. context and even for us who profess to be Christians. There are those who have attempted to demonstrate that Jesus wasn't talking about immigrants when in this passage from Matthew he uses the term "stranger." Some say that Jesus was talking about people different from us, and nothing more. These tend to be the same persons who argue that Jesus himself was not an immigrant. Jesus, however, grounds his teachings recorded in Matthew 25 in Jewish scripture. Those who heard him knew precisely what he was saying when he spoke of the stranger.

For Jesus, the term "stranger" had a very specific meaning. The stranger was the foreigner who came into one's community and to whom people of faith were to extend care. According to Leviticus 19:33, faithful care for the stranger required generous, if not extravagant, hospitality. The stranger was to be treated as if he or she was a native, a citizen. The stranger was never to be oppressed. Instead the stranger, the immigrant among God's people, was to be loved; loved even as we love ourselves. This is Jesus's own reference point when he says, "Welcome the stranger and you will welcome me." It is a mandate from God's own heart. God is the God of immigrants throughout the history of the community of faith.

The biblical story tells us that Mary and Joseph had to flee to the land of Egypt with the baby Jesus because of Herod, who was threatened by the birth of the Christ Child. Mary, Joseph, and Jesus were themselves immigrants, political refugees to be exact. They were not the first. We remember Abraham and Sarah as they gave their lives over to God, who led them out to a new land and a new life, for God's own holy purposes. We remember Moses, Aaron, and Miriam as they led the Hebrew people out of Egypt, and out from under their economic exploitation, their slavery. We remember the early Christians who traveled beyond the boundaries of home in order to share the good news of Christ Jesus. The biblical story is a reminder that immigration is as old as humanity, and a global issue. The whole of Christian scripture, and specific passages like Matthew 25, must be examined prayerfully, for they are our life guide. As I strive to understand how I am to respond to the one who is a migrant upon the earth and with whom I cross on the path of life, I am daily drawn to scripture, wanting to know more and more.

While doing research on the meaning and purpose of Matthew 25, I came across a commentary that suggests that while scripture in other passages talks about our sins of commission, those sinful things we do like lying, adultery, and killing, Matthew 25 focuses on our sins of omission; those things we fail to do, like failing to welcome the stranger. When I read this commentary, it did not sit well with me. On the surface of the passage I could see what the commentator was stating, but my gut was not at peace with his explanation of the passage. One morning, the reason for my discomfort surfaced in my mind. Matthew 25 is a passage about both omission and commission. We all too often fail to welcome the stranger—our sin of omission. The truth is, however, that our sins of commission have also all too often caused others to become strangers, immigrants among us.

Abundant are the studies that have shown the negative impact the globalization of the economy has had on people, particularly the poor. The North American Free Trade Agreement (NAFTA) and its devastating effect on the common Mexican corn farmer is worthy of our consideration. Before NAFTA, the twin plant projects, or the *maquiladoras,* that dotted the length of the U.S./Mexico border with production factories, took jobs from the manufacturing centers of the United States to this border. U.S. workers were left without jobs while desperately poor Mexican workers were recruited to take on their jobs in Mexican border communities at a pittance of pay and only long enough to fill the needs of the corporate coffers. Laid-off factory workers in the United States have become internal migrants, moving to other parts of the country seeking jobs, while Mexican workers first lured to the border area by the *maquiladoras* now find themselves crossing over into the United States as those factory jobs move to other parts of the world where workers willing to work at an even cheaper rate are found. In the process of economic expansion and exploitation, the poor are pitted against each other. These indeed are sins of commission. They may be the sins of corporations supported by governments that do not always seek the common good, but if we do not challenge the sins of corporations and unjust governments, then we are complicit in their sin.

There is also the sin of allowing immigrants to work in this country without the protection of our U.S. labor laws. Immigrants come to the United States because there are jobs here and, contrary to those who say that immigrants take the jobs of U.S. workers, economic studies have shown time and again that the United States needs and will continue to need immigrant workers. Yet we have failed to treat the immigrant worker fairly, with the opportunity to work for fair pay and without the looming shadow of the fearful darkness of being undocumented. As a country that speaks loudly of valuing family and loving children, how can we allow our U.S. government to separate families through the deportation of fathers and mothers who have simply been working in this country to feed their families? In states like Arizona, we must also ask ourselves how we can allow not only the economic exploitation of immigrants, but also the political exploitation of our immigrant brothers and sisters as politicians use them to gain votes, falsely accusing immigrants of being responsible for every social ill that this country faces. Even our language must change. Referring to immigrants as illegal aliens dehumanizes and ostracizes them.

Our sins for which Christ Jesus will judge us are sins of both omission—all those times we failed to welcome the stranger—and commission—all those times we allowed and even participated in the exploitation of others that forced them into the immigrant life and our exploitation of our immigrant brothers and sisters among us. The burden of our sin is heavy upon our shoulders, but I believe that the purpose of the parable of the Judgment of the Son of Man in Matthew 25 is not to make us fearful, but rather to extend gracious wisdom to us about how we are to live our lives.

One day I joined other bishops in San Diego, California. We wanted to see what was happening at that most south-western section of the U.S./Mexico border so we traveled through the city toward the sea, down to the border. We came as close as we could to a place called Friendship Park. Not that long ago Friendship Park was a historic gathering place for families—Mexican families and U.S. families. Sunday afternoon picnics were a part of the gift of this beautiful setting. Oh, but there was so much more.

Families who gathered at Friendship Park for Sunday afternoon picnics went there not only for the beauty of the place, or for the rest that lazy Sunday afternoons offered. Immigrant families have over the years gone to this park to be able to see their families across the border fence that divides the U.S. from Mexico. Many of these families are separated by national borders and by fences and walls that keep being built between the United States and our neighbor, Mexico, a symptom of our broken national immigration policy. At Friendship Park, some fathers were able to see their little children only through the fence, reaching as best they could through the links of the fence to touch the faces and kiss the hands of their precious children.

On the day we went to Friendship Park, though, we couldn't get in. It had been closed. A historic gathering place for families uniting north and south is now under the control of those who have been contracted by the U.S. Department of Homeland Security to build a wall that extends all the way out into the sea. That wall has been going up for a long time, and the builders needed to close down Friendship Park in order to finish building that wall out into the sea, a massive separator of families and countries that has brought a shadow upon this country as dark as night.

We stood at the edge of Friendship Park feeling the chill of that shadow of darkness, a silence overcoming us. But then we heard a mighty word of hope. We were told that while the wall's massive foundational pillars had been placed deep in the sea of the Pacific, the sea had refused to let those pillars stand. Through the power of its waters, the sea had pushed those pillars up and toppled them. In my mind's eye and with the ears of my spirit, I could see the mighty power of the sea, and hear its thunderous strength, and then it came to me.

If the sea could do that, what could we do as Christians if we allowed the waters of our baptism to flow out into the world, challenging all the pillars of injustice? If we would but follow the One in whose name we are baptized out into the world proclaiming that the reign of God has arrived, we could and we would topple the pillars of injustice, help lead the United States to just immigration reform, and with our immigrant brothers and sisters even welcome in the very reign of God!

After our visit, the building of the wall continued. I was taken aback when I returned to Friendship Park and saw not one but three walls being built. This time I was able to join others right at the wall in the heart of Friendship Park. From pictures I had seen of this particular wall, I could see that it was now different. A wall once imbedded with openings large enough for persons to reach through and touch hands is now covered with a thick mesh that allows only light and sound and glimpses of persons on the other side to come through. It is no longer physically possible to touch a person on the other side, but persons on both sides of the wall keep trying, placing the palms of their hands on the thick mesh to connect with a loved one on the other side. As they do this, I hear their expressions of love and encouragement for each other.

Walls can create a physical barrier between nations and persons, but they can never separate human hearts nor destroy the capacity of the human heart to persevere for what is right and just. I believe that by God's grace the walls of unjust immigration policies and practices and all that keep them standing will come tumbling down. I pray that people of good will and of faith will continue to work and wait for that day.

2 | Meeting at the Border

Restoring Human Dignity

Gerald Kicanas

Beginnings

I grew up on the North Side of Chicago in a predominantly Polish neighborhood. The Sisters of Nazareth, a Polish congregation, taught me in grade school, and when upset, they would talk to each other in Polish so we would not understand them. I remember wondering why everyone did not speak English. I only wished I could understand what they were saying. Maybe it was better that I did not.

I went to high school at Archbishop Quigley Preparatory Seminary in downtown Chicago. It was there that I first learned about cultural diversity. There I met classmates from all over the city and suburbs. They were of Irish, Polish, Lithuanian, Italian, and German background with a few Hispanics and African-Americans. I remember going home and saying to my mom, "Everyone at school is this or that. What is our nationality?"

She responded, "Lebanese, but don't tell anyone. They won't know what it means."

My grandparents came to this country from Syria and Lebanon as immigrants. My mother's family settled in St. Paul, Minnesota. Being very poor, they lived in the flats, a poor inner-city area one might call a slum. My grandfather was a traveling salesman who rode a horse-drawn wagon, selling silks in the Dakotas. My grandmother had her hands full with thirteen children—she lost two others. Both my mother's parents spoke Arabic and just a few phrases in English.

My mother, the youngest girl of that family, dreamed of going to college, but because her father believed that only boys needed higher education, she was not allowed to pursue that dream. It was a great disappointment in her life even as she celebrated her one hundredth birthday in 2012. Nevertheless, she and each of her siblings learned English, became educated, and benefited greatly from growing up in the United States.

My father had a twin sister who died shortly after birth. His mother died when he was very young. His father, an alcoholic, apparently overwhelmed by the prospect of caring for four children, placed them in an orphanage in Indiana. I never knew much about my father's family or of their story, but my father would often brag that his father was a priest. Actually, he was raised by Fr. Freiburger, who headed the orphanage.

My mother spoke Arabic, but my father did not. My sisters and I never learned the language of our heritage because when we were growing up Arab families preferred to integrate, leaving their language and culture behind (except for the food). In retrospect, I wish I had learned Arabic—a language that would serve me well now in my work with Catholic Relief Services.

As a Catholic priest in Chicago, I first served at a parish in Libertyville near the seminary I attended. After just two years as a priest, I went to teach at Quigley Seminary South, our high school seminary of eight hundred boys on the South Side of Chicago, where a number of our students were Hispanic. As their teacher, I wanted to know them better, to understand their language, and to appreciate more of their culture. While the students spoke English, their parents did not. I decided to go to Mexico to study Spanish. It was in Cuernavaca, Mexico, that I began to love and appreciate the Latino culture and became acquainted with the struggle many families faced in trying to provide for their children in Mexico.

Chicago is a richly diverse community. As auxiliary bishop in Chicago (1995–2001), I moved in and out of various ethnic and racial communities. I treasured those experiences but on occasion came upon people who found the experience of diversity upsetting, even threatening. While I came to value diversity, my experiences did not include the opportunity to become familiar with the question of immigration. It was not among the pastoral priorities where I served at the time.

Arrival in Arizona

On Friday the 13th of October 2001, I got a call from Archbishop Agostino Cacciavillian, the Apostolic Nuncio to the United States at the time. He told me the Holy Father had appointed me coadjutor bishop of the Diocese of Tucson in Arizona. I asked, "Pardon me?" I knew little about Tucson or the Southwest, but I was happy that I would get to use my Spanish.

I quickly learned that the Diocese of Tucson was among the largest geographic dioceses in the United States and that it included Tombstone, the town too tough to die, and Mission San Xavier del Bac, a splendid church, known locally as the White Dove of the Desert, and one of the early missions established by Padre Eusebio Kino, the great Jesuit missionary and explorer.

I heard for the first time of the Sonoran Desert, the vast territory of harsh desert, forests of giant Saguaro cacti, and "sky mountains" forested by oaks and ponderosa pines. I learned that the diocese includes Arizona's entire border with Mexico, from Douglas to Naco to Nogales to Sasabe to San Luis. I also became aware of the number of migrants from Mexico and Central and South American countries who died trekking through the desert alone or abandoned by ruthless smugglers called *coyotes*. The migrants sought only a better life in the United States. I felt immediately that these tragic deaths cried out for a pastor's response.

Change of Perspective

Two summers before I came to Tucson, I passed through the entrance gate to the camp at Auschwitz in Poland and read the chilling phrase, "Arbeit Macht Frei" (Work Makes You Free). I wandered the now-still streets of that concentration camp viewing the scuffed, unclaimed luggage, some marked with its owner's name. I saw the piles of worn shoes of every size, the locks of hair, the collections of combs, eyeglasses, and shaving utensils. I passed through the empty barracks and tried to imagine what it must have been like to live in them.

I saw the prisoners' faces only in the black-and-white photographs, yet still I stood shocked in disbelief. I stood before the wall where innocent people were shot. I passed through the horrific showers that spewed poisonous gas and stopped, stunned, by the furnaces.

How could the Holocaust happen? How did society stand silent and not shout out against such horrific crimes?

I also visited the concentration camp in Dachau, Germany. I stopped to read a letter written by a teacher, displayed behind glass. The letter urged teachers and parents to bring their children to Dachau so that they might see and be resolved never to let this inhumanity happen again.

Nothing is comparable to the Holocaust. It was an experience of raw evil, evil of the most blatant kind. There are other tragic experiences of human degradation to bring back the memory of that nightmare, even if those events pale in comparison.

For me, the deaths of people along the U.S./Mexico border echo a similar tragedy, in the loss of human life. Why does society allow these migrant workers to continue to die in the desert? The same inexplicable silence that allowed the Holocaust may well prevail over immigration as well.

Soon after I arrived in Tucson, I had the opportunity to go with a group of forty interfaith leaders—Jews, Christians, and Muslim—to visit Altar, Sonora, a Mexican city located about an hour south of the Arizona border. Thousands of migrants at that time came to Altar from various parts of Mexico and from numerous Central and South American countries. Altar was and is the staging area for migrants preparing to embark on their journey through the desert.

The magnitude of the migration at the time could be witnessed simply by walking the streets of Altar. Stores everywhere were selling backpacks, hiking boots, water bottles. The *coyotes*, human smugglers, lined the streets waiting to escort their "prey" across the border.

We came to witness the plight of migrants who were preparing for their trek north through the treacherous desert. I had no idea what to expect nor how moving and powerful an experience it would be.

Perhaps one can only understand the immigration issue by meeting someone trying to reach the United States. If someone listens to them, tries to understand their feelings and hear their dreams, the heart changes.

Unlike the migrants, we boarded a comfortable, air-conditioned bus to make the journey south across the border. We took the paved road, not the gravel one traveled by migrants who are stuffed into hot, dilapidated vans heading north from Altar through Sasabe and then into the promised land of the United States.

On our way to Altar we stopped in Magdalena, Sonora, at the burial site of the Jesuit missionary Eusebio Kino, S.J., who first brought the Gospel to Pimeria Alta—a Gospel that calls us to reach out to the smallest and weakest. I saw the bones of Padre Kino, now lying in a grand rotunda under a ceiling featuring a mural of Kino among the people he came to evangelize. Missionaries are never tentative, never hesitant. They live their lives as the archer shoots, their eye fixed on the target. They teach. They preach. They witness. They speak up and never stand by idle. They are people of action.

We arrived in Altar about an hour and a half later. We were to visit the Rev. René Castañeda, a young diocesan priest assigned by his archbishop to minister to migrants. Just that morning, twenty-two men, most about twenty years of age, had arrived in Altar from Chiapas. I saw their fearful faces as I passed among them, shaking their hands and asking, "¿Como se llama? ¿De donde?" (What is your name? Where are you from?) There was an immediate trust established by the collar I wore. "Su bendición, padre," they said, asking for a blessing.

When we stepped into the chapel there, I saw many young men kneeling, some holding images of Our Lady of Guadalupe. Many wore rosaries around their necks. They were seeking divine help for their journey.

After a brief conversation with Father René and his staff, we went to see the *casas de huespedes* (guest houses) built by people in Altar to accommodate the influx of people seeking a new way of life in the North.

It was there and then that one of my companions, a Jew, had a powerful insight that touched us all. He reflected with us that those crowded, congested *casas*, it seemed to him, felt as if we too had stepped through the gate at Auschwitz into a barracks—not in Poland or Germany—but in Mexico where sixty or more men, women, and children were stacked three-tiers high, two to a bunk, in a room no bigger than an ordinary size bedroom.

The black-and-white pictures of human degradation I remembered from Auschwitz and Dachau came back to me in color—with the real faces and terrified eyes I had seen here in Altar. I had shaken their rough, coarse hands. The stench, the filth, the squalor told me that human life was still being treated with less than the dignity any human deserved.

The sixty people, mostly men, mostly young, some only partially dressed, few with shoes, told us about their plight. They pay $2.50 to $5 a day to stay in this horrible hovel. Food is extra. They pay $1,800 to a *pollero* (smuggler) to guide them on their journey across the border. They want to work. They want to provide for their families. They want a decent human life—nothing extraordinary, nothing grand. They just want basic dignity and a chance to survive.

Some in America fear migrants as terrorists, criminals or "those illegals." But when you meet the people and talk with them, you see that they are human beings living desparate lives, seeking the same freedom our ancestors sought when they came through Ellis Island or some other port of entry into the United States. They love their children, enjoy eating, treasure friends, and want a stable way of life.

In what was the most touching moment for me, our group formed a circle around a large white cross placed at the beginning of the gravel road that leads to Sasabe. The cross commemorates 146 people—some of the many men, women, and children who have died in the desert along the Arizona border. As we concluded our prayer for these victims, a van filled with twenty-five people stopped. They asked for my blessing, knowing full well the dangers they faced. I broke down. But I could see that they were resolved to get to the United States, hoping to find a job and help their families.

On the way back to Tucson, we shared with one another our thoughts about our experience in the barracks and on the road. We came back determined not to remain silent, but to begin to clamor for comprehensive immigration policy change. Like Father Kino, who reached out to the smallest and weakest, we wanted to speak up and not stand by idle.

Encounter in Ambos Nogales

In the eleven years following that trip to Altar, I have met many more migrants: migrants waiting to begin their perilous trek; migrants working legally in the vegetable fields; migrants in detention, awaiting trials for illegal entry; and migrants just deported back to Mexico.

I met migrants in *ambos Nogales*—the twin cities of Nogales, Arizona and Nogales, Sonora, where several Jesuit priests and women religious work together in the Kino Border Initiative (KBI). In Nogales, Arizona, KBI works with college and university students seeking to learn more about the border. In Nogales, Sonora, KBI runs a *comedor*, a dining hall, for recently deported migrants and a shelter for women and children who have been deported. Their work provides safety and sustenance.

At the *comedor* men and women stood in a line to get breakfast. They carried their meager possessions in the plastic bags given to them by the Border Patrol when they were deported. Eating at the *comedor*, unlike the meals on their journey, provides a setting with some dignity. Here they are at tables, sitting with some comfort and civility. It was our privilege to serve them food, pour their lemonade, and take their plates after they had eaten.

We sat with them after the meal to listen to their stories: stories of terror, stories of being exploited, stories of dashed hopes.

"Where are you from?" we asked. They answered, "From Chiapas, from Sinaloa, from Saltilla, Vera Cruz, from Honduras, Guatemala, from Nicaragua."

"How old are you?" They were as young as nineteen. Most looked older than their age, their faces weather-beaten and worn.

"How many times have you tried to enter the United States?" For some it was their first time and some said they would never try again. It was so difficult, so frightening, so disappointing. Others had tried three or four times. Getting a job was their dream. Hope for a better life made it worthwhile to endure the suffering they experienced.

We visited *Casa Nazaret*, Kino Border Initiative's shelter for deported women and children. Seven women were living there as they planned for their future, all very young, most separated from their husbands and children. They told of the terror in their journey to enter the United States. They spoke of being robbed and beaten and of the danger of being raped. Despite the dangers, their dream was to be with their family in a place where they can have a decent way of life.

One woman was staying with her young son and daughter in the shelter cared for by the Sisters of the Most Holy Eucharist. As we were talking, the small boy—about seven years old—came over and took out a map which he spread out on the table. He showed us where he and his family had traveled from in the south of Mexico. He traced on the map the path they had followed. He showed each place they stopped along the way. "The bus was crowded and dirty. The walk in the desert so scary and so difficult. I was so thirsty," he said. Then he retraced the path back to the south of Mexico as he said, "They are making us go back."

Encounter in a Hospital

I met another migrant in a Tucson hospital. He was a young man, fifteen years old, from Chiapas, a poor state in the south of Mexico. He spoke only his native indigenous language, neither English nor Spanish. His uncle, who lived in Tucson, translated for him. He had climbed aboard a freight train, going el Norte (to the North) in hopes of finding a job to help his mom and seven siblings. He jumped from the moving train and as he fell beneath it, his legs were severed. Hospitalized, his dreams were crushed, knowing he would return home now dependent on the family he wanted to help.

Enounter in the Fields

Bishop Jose Guerrero Macias, bishop of Mexicali, and I met migrants in the fields in San Luis Rio Colorado, Mexico. We walked the fields with them and saw the backbreaking work they do every day. They arrive very early in the morning when the air is frigid. Surprisingly, most farmworkers are older—in their forties. I always reasoned migrant workers were young to do such difficult work.

They pick lettuce, onions, pomegranates, and other crops. The Yuma Valley is very fertile, the winter vegetable capital of the world. What would we do without them gathering the food that adorns our tables?

The work is tough, messy, exhausting. The pesticides can cause permanent health problems. But for these workers, it is a way of caring for their families.

We saw a group of twelve farm workers who waved at us from the side of the road in San Luis, Rio Colorado, Mexico. We stopped to talk to them. Most were young, some just fifteen or sixteen years old. They were placing irrigation pipes to get water to the recently planted seeds—hard work. Despite the heat, most were wearing sweatshirts to ward off the harsh rays of the sun. Although they seemed hesitant to talk with us, they told us they were paid $13 dollars a day and receive no health care or other benefits.

The fields stretched for miles: cotton, asparagus, corn, wheat, and green onions. We stopped at one of the onion farms and walked amid the multitude of people—men and women, adults and young people, all working side-by-side to bring in the harvest and to bundle the onions with rubber bands into the packets found later in U.S. grocery stores.

The onion pickers earn 25 cents per bundle of one dozen onions. They arrive in the fields at 2 a.m. and work until 4 p.m. I talked for some time to an older man, Delores, who has been working the fields since he was a young boy. He has eight children, four girls and four boys. All of them work in the fields, some for other growers. Asked why he keeps working at his age, his response was blunt and immediate: "So we can eat."

It breaks my heart to see the primitive housing in which the farm worker families live. Many homes are made of cardboard with no indoor plumbing. They are built along the road and the irrigation canals where the laborers wash themselves and clean their clothes.

The farm workers talked about the difficult circum-stances in which they have to work. One described how undervalued he feels—the packaged food that is the end result of their labor seems to be taken for granted. While everyone shops at grocery stores, few understand the hard work it takes to get those vegetables to the store counters.

They spoke of the long days, nearly always ten to twelve hours. They shared what it is like to be out in the field when the wind and rains come. They rush to get the tarp over the crops, but in the meantime, they get drenched and then sit, cold and wet, waiting for the rain to stop. Owners do not pay for time lost due to what is considered an act of God. So the workers go home with less money than they expected to care for their families. The combination of working next to hot machines and then getting wet and cold causes chills and sickness.

The workers also spoke of working with pesticides. One man mentioned that he regularly gets check-ups to make sure he is not getting sick. While workers are taught about the dangers of the pesticides, the pressure of the job leads many to ignore the precautions.

Encounter in a Federal Service Processing Center in Florence, Arizona

Once, on a visit to the Federal Service Processing Center in Florence, I had an epiphany about the strength and determination of the human spirit.

This facility is the largest of its kind and on the day I visited, there were upwards of eight hundred people from many nations and backgrounds being detained there. Migrants wait anxiously at the facility to hear the outcome of administrative or deportation processes concerning them. While there, they receive food and an opportunity for rest. If they were injured on their journey, they receive medical treatment.

For some of those present, this day's journey was no different from many trips north that end in detention at the facility. They are held at the facility for a few days, and then returned home to their country of origin. For some of the migrants, their deportation only results in another attempt to cross the border a few weeks or months later. They continue their efforts to enter the United States in search of steady pay—even if it means risking their lives on the journey to the "promised land." Should they finally cross the border into the United States, it means resources for their families back home, so the risks are endured again and again.

Those running the facility try to make it look less like a detention center. Someone thought to hang national flags from the dining hall ceiling, representing the migrants' countries. Despite the colorful flags, reminders of home, it is what it is: a stark detention facility. Men and women will continue to be stopped, sent to the facility, and returned home. Then, when their strength and resolve returns, some will try again.

It was clear to me that day that the drive to survive is strong. We can detain people forever, but we cannot contain or restrain the human spirit that moves people to seek a better way of life.

Encounter at the Border Wall

I stood with a group of young people on one side of a daunting steel fence at the Nogales Point of Entry on a Saturday afternoon one December. Archbishop Ulyses Macias, archbishop of Heromosillo, and a group of young people stood on the other side. There was a donkey in their midst, a young man holding it, tethered. A young girl dressed in white and blue sat on the donkey.

The two groups could see each other through the grate. We could hear singing in English on our side and in Spanish on theirs. Our combined chorus ascended the barrier as together we prayed for migrants who have died in the desert. Two young people, one on each side, approached the wall and exchanged white ribbons through a small hole, symbolizing our prayer for an end to the deaths in the desert.

We reenacted the Posada, the journey of a refugee family, Mary and Joseph, seeking a safe place to stay. After several rejections in which the family was turned away because there was no room, we passed through a gate to the Mexican side, gathering with our brothers and sisters in Mexico. We greeted one another and exchanged treats.

While ministry can be very frustrating at times, there are those moments—such as the Border Posada—of sheer delight. The young people who took part impressed me so much. They came to Nogales on both sides of the border because they wanted to pray, to give witness, to cease being strangers, to encounter new friends. They came to turn walls that divide into bridges that unite.

The Posada was one of many programs from a collaborative effort called Dioceses Without Borders involving the Archdiocese of Hermosillo in Sonora, Mexico, and the Dioceses of Phoenix and Tucson in the United States. This cooperation among dioceses has resulted in an opportunity to learn more about one another along the border and to respect and value one another.

All of these encounters have helped me put a face on migrants, to hear their voices, and to become even more determined to work for comprehensive immigration policy change.

Complexity

I know there are no easy or facile answers to the challenges of the border. Yes, there are good people, job-seeking men and women who are only looking for a decent way of life for themselves and their family, but there is also a criminal element that must be confronted along the border. As we move to comprehensive immigration reform, we need to secure the border from criminal behavior, end the violence and destruction of property along migrant routes, and address the human, drug, and weapons trafficking that are all too prevalent.

Securing the Border

Clearly our nation has a responsibility to secure its border, to know who is in the country and who is entering it. This becomes a momentous task when working with such a large and porous borderland.

Several years ago, Bishop Minerva Carcaño of the Desert Southwest Conference of the United Methodist Church and

I visited with Chief Michael Nicley, then head of the Tucson Sector of the U.S. Border Patrol. The visit was very helpful in allowing us to share our common concerns for ending the deaths in the desert and to address other pressing issues involving immigration into southern Arizona from Mexico and elsewhere.

As part of our visit, we toured the Nogales headquarters of the Border Patrol and drove with Border Patrol officers into the desert west of Nogales to experience what patrolling the border is like. I was impressed by the sensitivity of the Border Patrol officers. They realize the dangers in the desert for the migrants and for their fellow officers. The vast terrain makes surveillance difficult, and there are tragic results when people get lost or do not have sufficient provisions for the dangerous journey.

As we passed along the metal fence separating the United States and Mexico, it brought home to me how problematic being neighbors can become. Later, we sat in a Border Patrol van with its windows covered by bars as officers threw rocks at the vehicle to give us an experience of what their comrades sometimes encounter along the border. We saw how difficult it is to prevent drugs from entering the country, and we passed through the detention areas where migrants are housed as they await deportation later in the day.

My heart goes out to the Border Patrol agents who can be real heroes. Yes, there are patrol agents who act less than admirably, but many are trying to do an impossible task with great compassion.

Not only does the Border Patrol have the task of enforcing the unenforceable, it also has been charged with the unenviable task of stopping desperate people, then returning those desperate people into sometimes dire circumstances. On the other hand, Border Patrol officers also save lives by providing food and water to detainees they find lost in the desert—people driven to dangerous and unauthorized crossings as they seek ways to feed their families, or simply to reunite with loved ones.

I attended a funeral of a member of the Border Patrol who was killed by drug traffickers, run over mercilessly. What a tragedy for his young family. We need to pray for the safety of those charged with tending our borders. They do their work at the risk of losing their own lives.

As can happen in law enforcement, there are times that justice is not served. There are times when law enforcement can abuse its power. At such times it is important to raise concerns and expect that answers are provided and changes made.

At times, talking with deported migrants has revealed experiences of Border Patrol officers overstepping boundaries, responding inappropriately or using excessive force. I have found the leadership of the Border Patrol willing to hear concerns and, in many instances, to respond. It matters that violations of rights and diminishment of human dignity should be reported and addressed forthrightly.

Fear of Ranchers

Ranchers along the border also express fear and concern for their safety and that of their families. Rob Krentz, a rancher in our diocese and a Catholic, was a Good Samaritan for others. Rob would assist migrants who were almost dead on their feet, providing water and food and calling in rescuers if needed. In 2009, Rob was shot and killed, gunned down on his own property, probably by a drug trafficker. His wife, Sue, and their children were devastated. I saw the shock, the sadness, and the anger of their community when I presided at Rob's funeral. More than one thousand people gathered for the Mass in the Douglas High School gym.

Truly, the tragedy of his death gave way to his entrance into glory. He was a person who did much good for others. When he saw where love was needed, he responded, giving a drink of water to someone or helping fix a tire or providing some other kind of aid to a person in distress.

People who attended the Funeral Mass may have come with anger and fear, but I know they left with a powerful message from Susan: "We cling to forgiveness, demand justice, and stand strong in faith."

Drugs, Weapons, and Human Trafficking

The reality along the border presents many concerns. With increased enforcement along the border, criminal elements have become more and more involved in assisting migrants to enter this country illegally. This has led to mistreatment of migrants and, in some instances, sexual exploitation and violence perpetrated against migrants on both sides of the border.

Drugs and weapons pass along our southern border every day. This must be stopped. The power of drug cartels must be broken. Drug peddlers have even stooped to forcing children crossing the border to go to school in the United States to become mules, carrying drugs into our country.

Another crime occurring along our U.S./Mexico border is sex trafficking. This detestable crime is hard to detect, with victims who are unable or unwilling to report their abuse. We know it is happening, but the extent is hard to determine.

Any solution to the immigration issue must include increased security along the border to prevent the free-flow of weapons and drugs and the ability of unscrupulous people to engage in the sex trade.

Working for Comprehensive Immigration Policy Change

For the last eleven years we have heard from our presidents and legislators that our immigration system is broken. Indeed it is. Our country can do better in responding both to its need for workers and to the needs of people from other countries desperately searching for work.

President Barack Obama and the Congress, our elected officials, need to have the courage to act. The United States Conference of Catholic Bishops has for many years outlined the fundamental elements necessary for comprehensive immigration policy reform.

The U.S. bishops believe that a comprehensive immigration policy would help end illegal entry and help to focus energy on securing the border from criminal elements.

Illegal immigration is not good for anyone. It is not good for the migrant crossing the border. It is not good for a country to be unaware who is entering the country. The U.S. bishops want to replace illegality with legality.

What are the elements of comprehensive immigration reform?

First, comprehensive immigration policy change will include a pathway to citizenship for the 12 million or so people who are in the country illegally. This does not mean amnesty. Rather, comprehensive policy change that would include such a pathway would make demands of those seeking legalization. They would pay reasonable fines, learn English, and accept a provisional legal status as they go to the back of the line behind those who have applied legally to enter the country.

The U.S bishops, as well as others, believe that these requirements would ensure that migrants here illegally would earn their way to citizenship. It would permit the United States to continue to benefit from their hard work and would keep immigrant families together.

We cannot allow people to remain in the shadows, people who are contributing to our community and want nothing else but to be good and respectful members of our society.

In the shadows, they are being exploited. In the shadows, it is difficult for them to report the crimes and injustices they are experiencing. In the shadows, they live in fear of having some of their family deported.

Second, comprehensive immigration policy change will include a worker program allowing people to enter the country legally to do work needed here. It also will include worker rights such as equal wages and protection against indentured servitude. U.S. workers would have the first opportunity to apply for jobs, but migrants would have a chance if a U.S. worker is not found. We call this a future flow program.

What would a worker or future flow program do? It would ensure that migrants have a safe and legal pathway to work in the United States, protecting them from exploitation by smugglers, unscrupulous employers, and from death in the desert.

Finally, comprehensive immigration policy will support family unification. The Church is always concerned with the integrity of the family. Separation within families leads to societal problems. We need to find ways to keep migrant families intact. The family immigration system must be reformed so that families can reunify more expeditiously.

In addition, the U.S. bishops also have expressed strong support for legislative initiatives like the Dream Act and AgJobs, both of which could help improve the plight of migrants until there is a comprehensive immigration policy change.

We know what should be done. We know what needs to be done. Now it is time to get it done.

Contrary Voices

While I understand that people can hold contrary opinions in good faith, it has been painful to experience the anger and bitterness among Catholics and others toward those of us who call for immigration reform.

I remember being at a gathering in one of our diocesan parishes when SB 1070 was passed. This Arizona law that called for local police forces to check immigration status had been legally challenged but still was passed by the legislature. A man stood up at the gathering and said, "I resent you driving into Mexico using my donations to pay for your gas. I don't agree with your position on immigration. What is it about illegal you don't understand? I support SB 1070." Those present applauded his position. I have heard from parishioners in the diocese who feel strongly that the church should not become involved in these societal issues. I respectfully disagree.

A Need for Dialogue and Teaching

There is a great need for dialogue and teaching on what we believe as Christians and why the church is involved in issues like immigration.

There are many reasons why the church speaks out on immigration and issues that affect the dignity of human life. The preeminent reason is the scriptural and Catholic understanding of immigration. As Catholics, we read the scriptures as noting God's deep care and concern for the stranger, the sojourner, the outcast. Second, immigration is what I call an institutional issue, since it affects the life of the Church: its parish life, its programs, its growth and diversity. And third, immigration is a humanitarian issue, since it affects millions of persons, and thus has moral implications that the church is called to address publicly. There is a justice component to the immigration issue that must be achieved in order to protect human dignity.

Reflection on Scripture

In the Old Testament we hear Yahweh's preoccupation with the *anawim*, the little ones, the widow and orphans and the strangers. In Isaiah, we hear that we ought not harm or hurt the alien "for you yourselves were aliens in the Land of Egypt." The Israelites are exhorted not to wrong any widow or orphan or stranger. The Israelites are reminded that they were enslaved in Egypt, so they need to be sensitive to the basic needs of others and not to dismiss, exclude, or ignore them.

In Leviticus 19:33–34, the Israelites are reminded by Moses that they are to treat the stranger with respect and not molest him, as Moses describes the community they should aspire to become. "Count them as one of your own countrymen and love him as yourself."

Also in Leviticus we hear about the Jubilee Year in which God's people are to share their goods in God's name; after all, God alone is the God of all things. This text is filled with references to distributive justice, meaning that we will not hoard all for ourselves but share resources with those with great need.

In the New Testament, the experience of the migrant and the refugee is played out in the life of Christ, our Savior. Remember that Jesus was born in modest circumstances in a stable, since there was "no room in the inn." In his adult life, Christ was himself an itinerant preacher, who had no home (Matthew 8:20).

Jesus and his Holy Family were refugees as they fled to Egypt to escape the wrath of Herod (Matthew 2:13–15). They left their home out of fear for their lives, especially for the life of their son. The Holy Family experienced being strangers in a strange land. They felt the fear, the anxiety of being displaced. They were turned away and shunned. If they were on earth today, they would qualify as a refugee family under international law.

In the parable of the Good Samaritan, the person least expected to respond to the beaten and robbed man showed the most compassion. The priest in the parable looked away; so too the Levite, but the Samaritan saw the desperation of the man and chose to take care of him even at his own expense (Luke 10:25–37).

Jesus reminded his disciples (Matthew 25:31–46) that at the Last Judgment we will be judged not by what we own or what we have read but by what we have done. He told us that when we feed or clothe or visit the littlest and weakest among us, we do so for him.

Catholic Social Teaching

Catholic social teaching has a long and rich history in the Church. The heart of the Church's teaching is grounded in the dignity and sanctity of the human person from conception to natural death. Each person is entitled to live in conditions that enhance, not diminish, the dignity of human life.

The teaching of the Old and New Testaments have been expanded upon by popes and bishops through Catholic social teaching. In 2003, the bishops of the United States and Mexico issued a groundbreaking document titled *Strangers No Longer: Together on the Journey of Hope.* In that document, they outline the social justice principles pertinent to immigration:

First, "People have a right to find economic opportunities in their homeland."

Second, "Persons have the right to migrate to support themselves and their families."

Third, "Sovereign nations have the right to control their borders."

Fourth, "Refugees and asylum seekers should be afforded protection."

And finally, "The human dignity and human rights of undocumented migrants should be respected."

Papal teaching has been consistent in upholding the right of people living in abject situations to migrate in order to care for themselves and their family. Likewise, the Church consistently teaches that we must be committed to the exile, the alien, and the migrant. Each year, the Holy Father puts out a statement articulating this commitment and the underlying teaching on the dignity of all human life. In his 2010 statement, the Holy Father defended the "right to emigrate" as a fundamental right to leave one's country and enter another country to look for better conditions of life. The Holy Father's statement implies responsibilities among immigrants and the host countries.

> "States have the right to regulate migration flows and to defend their own frontiers, always guaranteeing the respect due to the dignity of each and every person. Immigrants, moreover, have the duty to integrate into the host country, respecting its laws and its national identity."

Conclusion

Immigration is a complex issue, but we cannot, as a nation, continue to avoid the effort it requires. A federal solution is needed, and needed now.

We must continue to educate the American public and our Catholic people about the need for a comprehensive and humane solution to this problem. As a moral matter, we cannot continue to exploit and dehumanize these, our brothers and sisters, who simply want to survive. As a nation, we cannot continue to accept their toil and taxes without offering them the protection of our laws.

I have been impressed by how pastoral leaders in all faith traditions share concern for the migrant. United we can find solutions to this complex problem.

Once while walking through the streets of Buenos Aires, Argentina, I noticed a sign written on a wall which read, *"Viva con pasion en cada instante de su vita. Sea feliz, suena y juntos construimos un future distinto."* Or, "Live with passion in every moment of your life. Be happy and hopeful and together we can build a different future."

I pray all of us will live our lives with passion and that we might dream of ways to improve and enhance our life together. While we face many issues and challenges in the United States, we can build a society where every human being is treated with dignity and respect. That is our dream and our mission that together we can make happen.

3 | "Something There Is That Doesn't Love a Wall"

Kirk Smith

It started out as a pleasant outing on a March morning in 2004. I had just moved to Arizona to become the fifth Episcopal bishop of the state, and had not even settled into my new home in downtown Phoenix when I was invited by the border missioner of the diocese, the Rev. Thomas Buechele, to join him and other interested Arizona Episcopalians on a bus excursion to Altar, Sonora, Mexico, about an hour south of the Arizona/Mexico border. Tom had organized this trip as a way of "putting a face on border issues." The issue of illegal immigration was just starting to receive increased national attention and Tom's hope was to give us an opportunity to meet and speak with some of the migrants preparing to cross the border as a way of countering the escalating inflammatory rhetoric.

And so I found myself on an air-conditioned tour bus headed toward the border town of Nogales, Arizona, sunscreen and picnic lunch in hand, destined for what I thought would be a day of sightseeing, Mexican food, the occasional educational or fact-finding stop, plus the chance to get to know some of my fellow travelers better. Little did I know that this trip was to change my ministry as well as change my heart.

My understanding of the complexities of border issues when I came to Arizona was very limited. Like many Americans, I was vaguely aware that our economy relies in great part on imported labor. Having lived in Los Angeles before moving to Arizona, I was used to the background patter of Spanish conversations and the knowledge that without cheap labor from Mexico, middle-class white Angelenos would have no one to mow their lawns, clean their homes, care for their children, or bus their tables when they dined out. I had also seen the wonderfully satirical movie *A Day Without a Mexican*, in which all Mexican labor mysteriously disappears overnight from Los Angeles, leaving the city in a state of economic and social collapse. But like most of my fellow Anglos, I believed that with some proper social engineering, diplomatic agreements, and increased border security, the problem could be solved.

But even before my trip across the border, my faith in such simplistic solutions was beginning to be shaken.

In the summer of 1995 I decided to make a serious effort to learn Spanish. I have always loved studying languages, but living in Los Angeles there was not much opportunity to use Greek or Latin, or even German or French. I enrolled in a church-sponsored two-week intensive course offered at a retreat center just outside Yosemite National Park. I didn't learn a lot of Spanish. (I remember that our time culminated with each participant preaching a sermon in

Spanish—I padded mine with such easily translated phrases as "Somos Christianos" and "Ama a tu projimo como a ti mismo." Fluent I was not!) What made more of an impression was being introduced to Latin American culture. One day during class we watched the 1983 Movie *El Norte*. This film, called "the Grapes of Wrath of our time" by film critic Roger Ebert, told the story of a brother and sister who leave the violence and poverty of their village in Guatemala to try to find a new life in America (*El Norte*—the North). After a harrowing journey, they establish themselves in Los Angeles, only to be subjected to the same kind of victimization they experienced in their homeland. It is a deeply moving and tragic tale, summed up in the line of one of the characters, "In our homeland there's no place for us; they want to kill us. In Mexico, there's only poverty. And in the north, we aren't accepted. When are we going to find a home, maybe only in death?"

I remember that when watching this scene, I had to run out of the classroom, overcome by sadness and shame. I stood outdoors in the beautiful sunlit pine forest with tears running down my face. Here I was, a clergyperson serving in Los Angeles, probably less than a half mile from where these scenes were filmed, and yet I was oblivious to the suffering that was literally on my doorstep. I resolved then and there to learn more about the plight of my neighbors who, until that moment, might as well have existed in a different universe.

Although the suffering of undocumented people was beginning to penetrate my consciousness, I did not really have any personal experience of it. The church I served in Los Angeles, St. James on Wilshire Boulevard, was only blocks from "the barrio," but it was well insulated by the lush lawns and high walls of Hancock Park, an area valued by Hollywood film executives for its nearby art museums and New England village–style shopping. It occurred to me briefly to try to offer a Spanish language worship service, but I was persuaded that this would be too much of a strain on our already overused physical plant.

It was not until I was elected Episcopal bishop of Arizona in 2004 and moved to this border state that I found myself at the epicenter of the immigration furor. Before I even sat down in my new office chair, what I had heard in the media became a physical reality.

In February of 2004, my wife and I moved into the bishop's house located next to the Episcopal cathedral in downtown Phoenix. Moving into a new life is always stressful, so we decided that after settling the house we would take a short vacation to recover. We had found a guest ranch located in Sasabe, Arizona, a tiny town right on the Mexican border, famous for its relaxed atmosphere and southwest cuisine. We enjoyed the trail rides in the desert, but were shocked by the amount of debris and trash scattered everywhere—plastic water bottles, discarded clothing of all sizes, empty food cans and plastic garbage bags, the flotsam and jetsam of hundreds, if not thousands, of men, women, and children on the run.

When the day came for the drive back to Phoenix, we left the ranch early in the morning, winding our way down the long dirt access road back toward the main highway. As we crept along, avoiding potholes and washed out sections of the road, I suddenly saw something out of the corner of my eye—a dark shape moved in the bushes by the side of the road. My first thought was that it was an animal, perhaps a *javelina* (a kind of wild pig), or maybe even a mountain lion. But no, it was a man—young, ragged, and obviously afraid. He was not afraid of us, but of a large green and white Border Patrol truck that had just crested the ridge of the road in front of us. I slowed down, overcome by a conflict. Oddly, my first thought was to wave to the Border Patrol agent and shout "He's over here!" as though this were some kind of childhood game of hide-and-seek. But then it hit me—this was a hunt, a manhunt, and I was standing between the hunter and his prey. Our men in uniform, the representatives of my country's government, were tracking and hunting human beings, and I was caught in the middle.

I don't know if that young man was ever caught. I tried not to look in his direction and thereby give the agent a hint as to his whereabouts. My guess is that he had already been spotted by the Border Patrol helicopter and that the agent was merely waiting for us to get out of the way should there be any violent resistance. But that image of a human being crouched in terror by the side of the road while I drove past will haunt me forever. The story of the Good Samaritan leaped to mind. Like my biblical counterparts, the priest and Levite of the story Jesus told, I had passed by my brother in need on the high road to Jerusalem.

And now, a few months later, I found myself on another road, the Sonoran Highway, on the journey from Nogales, Arizona, to the village of Altar. On the way, we stopped at the town of Magdalena for a rest stop and a chance to visit the grave of Eusebio Kino, the Jesuit missionary who served this area of the Sonoran desert for nearly thirty years and died in this place in 1711. His remains were rediscovered by archae-ologists in the 1960s and a museum and civic shrine had been built over his skeleton. Fr. Kino was later to become a "patron saint" for me. His missionary zeal, along with his genuine advocacy for the rights of native people against their Spanish colonial masters, won him the respect of Arizonans and Mexicans alike. I believe his spirit was with us that day as we headed deeper south toward Altar.

Altar is a hot and gritty town sustained by human misery. Its economy is fueled by the sale of items immigrants might need for their desert crossing—water bottles, hats, food, backpacks. Everywhere we looked, camping equipment and supplies were being hawked by street vendors. Other providers we did not see, like the aptly named *coyote*s, the guides who charge exorbitant fees to smuggle desperate people through the weak points in the border defenses and deliver them to "drop houses" in cities like Tucson and Phoenix. More often than not these *coyotes* victimize their customers, robbing or perhaps raping at gunpoint, or simply abandoning them in the desert once they had taken their money or if their charges had become weary, slow, or sick in the desert heat.

In the Altar town square, relying on those in our group who knew enough Spanish to ask questions, we visited with wary young men, boys really, older men, even a young family with small children, as they all prepared to cross the desert. We felt their terror at the grueling trip mixed with hope for the new life of their dreams. We saw the information posted in the local church about how to make the crossing safely and how to protect oneself from dehydration and poisonous snakes. We had a simple meal of enchiladas and black beans at a shelter sponsored by several church groups that were working hard to provide food and beds for these most desperate refugees.

The most moving part of our trip was a visit to a *casa de huespedes*. We might call them "hostels," although the old label "flophouse" seems more apt. For $2 a day, a refugee headed north can get a plate of *frijoles* and a bed of sorts in a rack of dormitory bunks, long sheets of plywood shelves, about six to a wall. When I went in these rooms and saw the gaunt and grimy men (and they are almost all young men) standing next to bunks stacked with their parcels of meager possessions, I could only think of the pictures taken by Allied troops when they entered the concentration camps of Auschwitz and Dachau near the end of World War II.

Our translator led us out into a rough-hewn courtyard where about twenty men were doing their best to rest and wash themselves from a trickle of water from an outdoor faucet. She explained to them that we were from a church group, and that we wanted to learn more about them and their journey. She assured them that they could trust us.

The men crowded around; some leaned down from a second story balcony. All wanted to talk.

I started by asking them, "Where do you come from?"

"From Guatemala," they replied together. "We are from the same village."

"And how did you get here?" I responded.

"We walked."

"Walked?" I said incredulously, "How far is that?"

"It was very long, about 1200km," one young man said. "It was difficult, some turned back, one died along the way."

"But *why* did you come?" I wanted to know.

"Our families are starving; there is no work for us in our village." They all nodded their heads in agreement.

"Where are you going?"

Several chimed in, "We don't know. Any place there is work."

"What kind of work do you want to do?" I asked, and their answer was simple:

"Anything."

"Why are you staying in this place? Are you waiting to cross?" Someone from my group asked.

"We tried," said one of the older men, "But two of our group got caught by the Border Patrol, so rather than leave them, we all turned ourselves in and came back together."

"What happens now?" was the inevitable next question.

"We wait until we can get enough money to try again."

At that point, one of the younger men, perhaps he was sixteen or eighteen, had a question for me. "Was I a priest? If so, could I say a prayer for them?"

For one of the very few times in my life as a clergyperson, I literally did not know what to say. We bowed our heads. All I could hear was the dripping of the water tap and the flies buzzing in the hot sun. I opened my mouth a few times, but nothing came out. I felt dizzy and disoriented. This was no place for rote platitudes or sentiments. I finally croaked out something about God being with us in our suffering, but my words, at least to me, rang hollow. We shook hands all around. I was not the only one with tears. As we got on the bus for our trip back to Phoenix, I knew that a more important journey for me was just beginning.

Thus when I began my official tenure as bishop in October 2004, I decided to make immigration a major focus of my episcopate. I felt I needed to do my best to be a public voice for those people I had met. I knew this would not be easy. Episcopalians make up only a tiny part of the population of Arizona. We officially number about 25,000, although I suspect that this is a generous estimate. We have about sixty-five congregations scattered over more than 800,000 square miles, so it is not always easy to find the local Episcopal Church. Demographically, Episcopalians tend to be better educated and wealthier than the average American. That is the good news. The bad news is that our average age is sixty-two. All these factors tend to make us "establishment types," not always given to high-visibility or controversial social stands. Although Arizona Episcopalians tend to be more progressive than the average voter (especially in liberal bastions like Tucson), I occasionally receive angry mail from parishioners who believe that the best solution to our immigration problem is to round up anyone who has brown skin or speaks Spanish and ship them back across the border.

But I was now convinced that there was only one response open to us as Christians, and that is the way of compassion, understanding, and care of the "stranger among us." I have never pretended to have a solution to what is an extremely complex problem, but I knew that any solution had to be one which, in the words of our baptismal promises, "respects the dignity of every human being."

The religious and theological foundations for this position have been stated many times, and my colleagues in this book will no doubt state them more eloquently than I. But it is worth revisiting them again as a way of making clear that insistence on a just and humane immigration policy is not merely the product of political expediency, nor is it even an issue of "civil rights" (although it may be both of those, too); rather, it is guided by the following biblically based assumptions:

1. A doctrine of creation outlined in Genesis in which human beings are created in the image of God (Genesis 1:27). The concept of "the brotherhood of man" is not therefore just some politically correct slogan, it is a *mandate* that we *must* care for each other as fellow daughters and sons of the same Creator. This idea is not unique to Christians, but is shared by every major world religion and is the starting premise of every moral ethical system.

2. The story of the People of God is a story of immigration. Abraham was an illegal immigrant; the people of Israel were "aliens" during their sojourn in Egypt, and unwelcome refugees when they fled to the land of Canaan. Jesus too could be considered an "undocumented person" during his childhood exile in Egypt. A rabbi wrote recently that Jews intuitively understand what it means to be undocumented. "It's a pitiable story. Abraham and Sarah lie and humiliate themselves to try to survive in a foreign nation they have not received permission to enter. It must have been agonizing. It's a story of strangers in a strange land, without protection, without connections and without a right to go about their business unmolested. It's an illegal immigrant's story. Judaism's whole history is one of not having a country of their own, of living as non-citizens in places where they were likely to be expelled at any moment."[1]

3. The Leviticus Holiness Code is emphatic about compassionate treatment of strangers living among us. Here the Old Testament becomes even more specific as it looks

---

1   Maurice Harris, "Abraham, Sarah, and the Arizona Law," The Oregonian, May 3, 2013.

back to the time when the people of Israel were aliens in a strange land. Its ethical teaching is based on this experience of exile. Our behavior toward the aliens must mirror the behavior of God toward his people when they, too, were in exile. "You must be holy, because the Lord your God is Holy." More specifically, Leviticus 19:33–34 (NRSV) reads, "When an alien resides with you in your land, you shall not oppress the alien. The alien who resides with you shall be to you as the citizen among you; you shall love the alien as yourself, for you were aliens in the land of Egypt. I am the LORD, your God."

4. Jesus's ministry was to the outcasts—to those marginalized within his own society: the physically and mentally ill, those who were ritually unclean (think lepers), women and children, those living morally questionably lives (think the woman at the well), as well as members of racial and religious minorities (think Samaritans). As we might expect, Jesus's association with such groups earned him the opprobrium of the establishment types ("he eats with tax collectors and sinners!"), the law-abiding ("he heals on the Sabbath!"), the political insiders ("we have no king but Caesar!"), and those whose careers were dependent on the cultural and civil status quo (Pharisees and Sadducees). Jesus's whole ministry was countercultural, and that position cost him his life. We might say his entire mission was on *la frontera*.

5. The early church grew by integrating those on its margins. This is the theme we hear in the struggle to incorporate Gentiles into what was originally a Jewish movement, as recounted in the book of Acts. Could non-Jews be part of God's saving plan? For Paul and his followers, the answer was a resounding "Yes!"

6. The missionary success of Christianity was based on adapting the Gospel into entirely new cultural contexts. Those of us who are of northern European descent are here because Roman missionaries like St. Augustine of

Canterbury were able to adapt his message to an indigenous pagan Anglo-Saxon culture. Gregory the Great advised Augustine to accommodate and thus convert. This lesson has been repeated again and again through the missionary history of the church.

So my "conversion experience" that hot day in Altar, Sonora, was a coming together of what I claimed to believe as a Christian and the natural compassion I felt for those young men and their families. It involved both my heart and head, my emotions as well as the teachings of my faith, what I knew Jesus would want me to do and that which, as a moral human being, I was compelled to do.

In the years that followed my trip to Altar, there have been many occasions for me to live out my new conviction. Nationally, there was increased attention to immigration issues. Fueled in those days by a booming U.S. economy, as many as a million people a year were crossing the Mexican border seeking jobs, plentiful amidst the growing suburban sprawl of the Sunbelt. Nor was the hunger for cheap labor limited to border states. By 2005, nearly every state in the country had significant populations of undocumented people—nearly 12 million in total. Oddly, this included even Hawaii, not exactly an easy destination to reach from the Mexican border! I remember, for example, attending a church conference in the picturesque small southern city of Asheville, North Carolina, and while waiting at the airport to claim my luggage, hearing announcements over the public address system in both English and Spanish!

But there was a dark component to this employment engine. Along with the American economy's growing dependence on undocumented workers, there was a concomitant suspicion that these very workers were becoming a threat to the American way of life. They were perceived as parasites on the social service structure, crowding out paying patients in hospital emergency rooms, burdening already

overcrowded public school classrooms, and even contributing to rising crime rates. Despite the fact that many studies
have indicated that such undocumented workers brought
far more *into* the economy than they took *out*, it didn't seem
to matter as the xenophobic attitude of many Americans
was ratcheted up, often by self-serving politicians and the
"schlock-jocks" of talk radio.

One very visible expression of this increasing tension was
the evolution of the Wall. When I was growing up in Arizona
in the 1960s, Arizona border towns were a popular destination for tourists and locals alike. The border checkpoints
were usually nothing more than a guardhouse peopled
by agents who casually waived people and cars across the
border on their way to shopping and great restaurants in
places like Nogales and Douglas. Ironically, the only real
obstacle to free travel was the suspicion Mexicans officials
sometimes had about Americans going *into* Mexico! Once,
when my father and I were invited to join a friend for some
fishing at the resort town of Puerto Penasco, about eighty
miles south of the border on the Gulf of Lower California,
my dad, a clergyman, was warned to list his occupation on
his travel visa application as "teacher," since the Mexican
government was wary about religious groups and "agitators"
causing social unrest in their country! How things have
changed!

But the Wall soon become a very dramatic example of the
increasing tension and distrust between our two countries.
About six years ago, our border missioner, the Rev. Seth
Polley, organized a border procession between the small
towns of Naco, Arizona, and Naco, Sonora. The climax
of that event was an interfaith service of the Eucharist in
which bread and wine were passed back and forth between
the bars of the fence separating us. That is now impossible, for every year the fence has become more elaborate
and fortified. There are now two twenty-one-foot-high steel
fences topped by razor wire, separated by a no-man's-land

about fifty feet wide, and patrolled electronically from high tech surveillance towers. Helicopters and spotter planes make occasional flybys and in nearby Sierra Vista, a large tethered blimp floats hundreds of feet above the desert floor, peering into Mexico with a top-secret combination of infrared and ground radar detectors. The Wall, which stretches to the horizon from east to west, is now nearly six hundred miles long, about the distance from New York to Chicago, and is guarded by about twenty thousand Border Patrol agents. Something like eight thousand immigrants have died trying to cross the Wall, many times the number that died at the Berlin Wall. Every time I see it, I think of President Reagan's challenge to the premier of the Soviet Union in 1987, "Mr. Gorbachev, tear down this wall!" Later the president said that his speech had been inspired by something he had seen spray-painted on the Berlin Wall: "This wall will fall. Beliefs become reality."

Three years ago, I was asked to speak at this border procession, now an annual event. I remembered other words about walls that separate peoples, the story of the wall of Jericho found in the book of Joshua (6:1–27). Most of us know the story from the old spiritual, "Joshua fit the battle of Jericho . . . and the walls come a-tumblin' down." The actual account is no less stirring:

> Now Jericho was shut up inside and out because of the Israelites; no one came out and no one went in.
>
> The LORD said to Joshua, "See, I have handed Jericho over to you, along with its king and soldiers. You shall march around the city, all the warriors circling the city once. Thus you shall do for six days, with seven priests bearing seven trumpets of rams' horns before the ark. On the seventh day you shall march around the city seven times, the priests blowing the trumpets. When they make a

long blast with the ram's horn, as soon as you hear the sound of the trumpet, then all the people shall shout with a great shout; and the wall of the city will fall down flat, and all the people shall charge straight ahead." . . .

On the seventh day they rose early, at dawn, and marched around the city in the same manner seven times. It was only on that day that they marched around the city seven times. And at the seventh time, when the priests had blown the trumpets, Joshua said to the people, "Shout! For the LORD has given you the city." . . . So the people shouted, and the trumpets were blown. As soon as the people heard the sound of the trumpets, they raised a great shout, and the wall fell down flat; so the people charged straight ahead into the city and captured it.

This passage was the basis of my sermon to those gathered on both sides of the border that day, for the message seems clear:

God hates walls!

We, however, love walls—we think we can use them, whether physical, social, or economic, to protect us against perceived enemies. But God does not like brothers and sisters to be apart—and whenever we put up walls against each other, God knocks them down!

As the prophet Isaiah reminds us: "For the LORD of hosts has a day against all that is proud and lofty, against all that is lifted up and high . . . *against every high tower, and against every fortified wall*" (2:15).

This was true with Jericho, with Hadrian's Wall, the Great Wall of China, with the Berlin Wall, and with every effort we make to keep people apart. They all ended up the same way—as piles of rubble.

I was reminded of that wonderful poem by Robert Frost "Mending Wall," in which a farmer, surveying the stone wall he so carefully repairs each year which then mysteriously collapses, concludes:

> Something there is that doesn't love a wall,
> That wants it down.[2]

That something or someone is God. God does not love a wall—God wants it down.

Christians might even go so far as to say that part of Jesus's message and ministry was to break down the walls that separate people from each other and from God—"making peace through the blood of his cross" (Colossians 1:20).

Those of us in the church who find the Wall on our southern border to be both an insult to our common humanity and a blasphemy against God believe that we, like Joshua, must make a great shout—to say to the world in the name of our faith—"tear down these walls!"

How then does God knock down walls?

We can learn from the story of the walls of Jericho. The answer is: *carry the ark, blow the trumpet, and raise a great shout.*

What does it mean to carry the ark?

First, that our purpose in opposing unjust walls at the border is not simply about justice—it is a religious campaign. Joshua carried the ark of the Lord around the walls, and so must we. In the campaign to get a humane border policy, we will need to keep on the high road of the spirit. There are excellent economic reasons for advocating a new immigration policy. There are excellent humanitarian reasons as well for eliminating restrictions that tear families apart and that foster unjust treatment of workers. But our task as religious leaders goes beyond those reasons. Ours

---

2 Edward Lathem, ed., *The Poetry of Robert Frost* (New York: Holt Reinhardt Wilson, 1975), 33.

is a spiritual and moral task—to say over and over again—
"this is not the way that God created his children to live—
this is morally wrong—God hates walls!" We must not forget
to oppose the walls of injustice with the ark of our faith.

Second, Joshua and his men were told to march around
the city of Jericho for seven days and seven nights. In other
words, they had a plan and it was, we would say, a long-
term plan. It did not promise any immediate gains. It was
a plan that required patience and perseverance, and yes, a
careful and deliberate strategy. It was not enough to rally
the troops and say—"go get 'em!" It took time, and it took
preparation and coordination.

The plan included trumpets. It was the noise from the
trumpets and the stomping of feet that caused the cracks in
the walls and their eventual collapse. Likewise, every victory
achieved in this country against oppression has required
people to make a great deal of noise; not only to write letters to the paper, or to preach sermons, but quite literally
to take to the streets. As religious leaders, we know that
prophetic action has always meant public protest. Just ask
any of the Old Testament prophets: they knew the power
of street drama and were not afraid to use it. That tradition has continued in this country from the time of the
Boston Tea Party to the March on Selma, from the March
on Washington to the antiwar protests of the Vietnam era,
to rallies for gay rights and living wages. Effecting change
means putting our lives and reputations on the line, and
it may mean that some of us must be willing to follow in
that tradition of civil disobedience of Mahatma Gandhi and
Martin Luther King Jr., but which goes back to Jesus himself. Blowing the trumpet is not something most of us religious leaders are used to doing. We tend to prefer the more
soothing sounds of organ and harp, but blow the trumpets
we must if the wall is to come down.

And I concluded my sermon: "The noise we make today
might not be a very big one, but I promise you that in the

days to come it will get louder and louder and that one day, those border fences will be like the wall of Jericho—nothing more than a collection of rubble. The politicians who build those walls might call themselves Christians, they might call themselves religious, but they didn't read their Bible—they forgot that God hates walls! And if that is true, then this wall doesn't stand a chance—for the trumpets will blow and the people will raise a great shout, and down this wall will come, and great will be the fall of it!"

My words to that group came about the same time that there was increasing legal pressure on some of my own undocumented parishioners in the diocese. A few years ago, it seemed as though the federal government was going to do the right thing by creating a humane border policy. The "McCain/Kennedy bill" looked like a possible way forward. But then came the recession and with it an increased level of fearfulness and paranoia. When proposed federal initiatives failed to get the required support, it was left to individual states to fill the vacuum through local legislation, much of which was punitive and targeted immigrants solely on race. The Arizona legislature passed several bills that would make it hard, if not impossible, for undocumented people to have access to social services and punished employers who knowingly employed them.

Much of this persecution was driven by politicians who were clever enough to ride this growing wave of suspicion and resentment. In Arizona, two notable examples stand out. The first is Maricopa County Sheriff Joe Arpaio, the self-styled "toughest sheriff in the West" who already had a reputation for unconventional, and, many would argue, inhumane treatment of prisoners. County jail inmates (a number that has more than doubled under his administration) are forced to wear pink underwear and to live in unair-conditioned "tent cities," where temperatures can reach as high as 130 degrees in the summer, and, until the courts intervened, were fed a diet of moldy bread and rotten fruit. Arizona civil rights groups have been vocal in their criticism of his tactics. Says local writer Jana Bommersbach, "Every time I watch Sheriff Joe unleash his 'posse' on another neighborhood with a high Hispanic population, arresting people with brown skin for the most stupid of offenses—honking their horn, having a tail-light out, not signaling when they change lanes—I have to wonder how anyone could not see this as an assault on an entire race of people." The *New York Times* agrees, writing in an editorial, "The sheriff says he is keeping the peace, but it seems as if he is doing just the opposite—a useless, reckless churning of fear and unrest." And yet in spite of these criticisms, grand jury investigations, and lawsuits against him which have cost taxpayers more than $40 million dollars, Sheriff Joe is consistently returned to office.

Sheriff Joe's political counterpart until recently was State Senator Russell Pearce, who represented a largely Mormon and heavily Republican district encompassing much of Mesa, Arizona. Pearce once worked with Joe Arpaio in the Sheriff's office and shares his political philosophy, which has been documented to have been influenced by several white-supremacist and neo-Nazi groups. Since 2004 Pearce has headed efforts to persecute and deport undocumented workers in the state.

That was the year in which he proposed Arizona's Proposition 200, which requires individuals to produce proof of citizenship when they register to vote or apply for public benefits. In that year, his crusade also took a personal turn when his son Sean Pearce, a sheriff's deputy, was shot and wounded by an illegal immigrant while delivering an arrest warrant.

What gained Pearce national attention was his sponsorship of Arizona SB 1070, which passed into law in April 2010 as the Support Our Law Enforcement and Safe Neighborhoods Act. The measure is the strictest anti-illegal immigration measure in decades within the United

States. After the Obama administration challenged the law, resulting in a federal court ruling that most of the law was unconstitutional, Pearce shot back at a gathering of conservative activists, "When you talk about *jihad*, that is exactly what Obama has against America, specifically the state of Arizona."

In a recent story on NPR, he was quoted as saying, "I believe in the rule of law. . . . I've always believed in the rule of law. We're a nation of laws"; and "I will not back off until we solve the problem of this illegal invasion. Invaders, that's what they are. Invaders on the American sovereignty and it can't be tolerated." The future of SB 1070 is still unclear, although the recent decision by the Supreme Court has probably weakened its impact by striking down it most punitive provisions.

After launching SB 1070, Pearce sponsored Arizona SB 1097, also debated by the legislature during the 2010 term, which would have especially targeted the children of undocumented people. Among the provisions of the new law:

- School districts would be required to identify and count all students who are in the United States illegally.
- The State's Department of Education would be required to report annually on the impact and costs to state taxpayers of the enrollment of these students.
- The State Superintendent of Public Instruction would be authorized to withhold state aid from districts that do not comply with the law.

To top everything off, Pearce even proposed a measure that would deny U.S. citizenship to children born in this country to illegal immigrants (so-called "anchor babies") even though such a law would be unconstitutional, as the 14th Amendment guarantees citizenship to anyone born in the United States. As of this writing, the Arizona legislature seems inclined not to take up such extreme measures. Senator Pearce apparently went too far for even his staunchest supports, for he was recalled from office in 2011, the first time this has happened in Arizona history, although at this writing there are rumors that he may run again. Other states, notably Georgia and Alabama, have already enacted similar measures, and it seems likely that Senator Pearce has unleashed political forces that will continue to play a major role in upcoming state and national elections as well as the recent (2013) bipartisan efforts to produce national immigration reform.

Some of my parishioners were on the receiving end of Sheriff Arpaio's policies on Good Friday, 2009. I was driving home from a visitation in southern Arizona when I got a cell phone call from our Hispanic minister, the Rev. Carmen Guerrero. She was calling from San Pablo Church, a Spanish-speaking congregation located in central Phoenix. She reported that "Sheriff Joe" had set up one of his mobile command centers directly across the street from the church, and that parishioners of San Pablo were afraid to come to Good Friday services for fear that they would be detained or arrested.

I immediately headed for the church, and when I got there found the situation as she described it to me. The church was set up for services, but there were only a handful of people present, and most of them were wandering around dazed, unsure what to do. I walked across the street and asked to speak to the officer in charge. "Do you know what day it is?" I asked. "Why was this particular location selected?" "Do you realize that you and your men are intimidating people from worship and thus possibly violating their First Amendment rights?" The deputy was very polite, but he was also insistent that he had his orders and could not help me. His only suggestion was that if I had a problem, I write the sheriff a letter of complaint. I later discovered that Sheriff Joe had gone one step further in other locations in the Phoenix area, and had actually sent his deputies onto church property looking for "criminals." So much for the ancient right of sanctuary! It was later disclosed that the sheriff's "Freedom patrols" had cost the taxpayers hundreds of thousands of dollars and had resulted in only a handful of arrests.

Throughout this whole episode I could think of only two things. The irony that the sheriff should have picked this holy day for his attack (thus equating himself with a more ancient law enforcement agent—Pontius Pilate), and the possibility that by my confronting his officers, I might be arrested. This was the first time that such a scenario had ever crossed my mind. It would not be the last.

In the years that have followed that confrontation, the pressure for immigration solutions from both sides increased. Arizona finds itself more and more in the national spotlight, due both to the sheer number of undocumented people crossing its border as well as the often dramatic efforts to address the problem from both sides of the political spectrum. From the right, there has been increased pressure from nativist groups such as the Minutemen, a vigilante organization that for a short time placed its armed members on the border. In the cities, the number of public demonstrations increased. Hispanic workers marched by the thousands on the State Capitol while their protests were echoed in other states as well.

One instance where this conflict was played out in the Diocese of Arizona was in Church of the Good Shepherd, located in the upscale retirement community of Cave Creek. The then-rector of that parish, the Rev. Glenn Jenks, had a long-term commitment to the plight of poor Spanish-speaking workers, having served as an immigration attorney before ordination (his license plate reads FRNLAW). Fr. Jenks was aware of the practice in his community of hiring undocumented workers, who usually would loiter about the local paint or hardware store waiting to be hired for day jobs, a practice that often resulted in abuse or unpaid wages.

He created a day worker center at his church where day laborers could come for safety and support and which acted as a clearinghouse for potential employers. The workers themselves took ownership in this project by donating a dollar a day to a fund that was used to provide medical and dental care for the workers and their families. The workers could also count on a meal of coffee, leftover pastries from the local Starbucks, and other items from the local United Methodist and Roman Catholic churches. In this way, about one hundred men and their families were helped on a regular basis. This was a courageous thing to do in the midst of a politically conservative, mostly white community, and Fr. Jenks and his congregation quickly found themselves at the center of a firestorm of controversy, with the editor of the local newspaper functioning as the vocal leader of the opposition. Fr. Jenks was labeled as "The Bad Shepherd," and his congregation and those they served were subjected to much verbal abuse. Their efforts, however, were not overlooked by the local and national media, and as a result, they were one of the first targets for Sheriff Joe, who brought his command center vans to Cave Creek in January 2008. He positioned his deputies' cars just outside the entrance to the church parking lot and stopped any car with an Hispanic-looking person in it for any tiny traffic violation, and in some instances, with no legal cause at all. The deputy would let the driver of the car go and arrest the Hispanic worker. That ended the program. This happened even before SB 1070 became law.

SB 1070 was a turning point for the nation, the state, and for the Episcopal Church. Even though the fate of this bill is not certain in light of the recent Supreme Court decision, it served as a model for other states that wished to rush into the power vacuum caused by lack of coherent federal lawmaking. Several states now have proposed SB 1070–inspired legislation, some of which make the provisions of the Arizona law look tame in comparison. Those on the other side of the issue attempted to boycott Arizona by taking their tourism business elsewhere, an effort which cost the state millions of dollars, even though it had no official support by any group, including the majority of Arizona religious communities. Meanwhile in the Episcopal Church, there was growing interest about what was happening in Arizona, and how the larger church might respond.

It was against this background that the Episcopal Church's House of Bishops (one of the two governing bodies of the Episcopal Church) decided to hold its annual fall meeting in September 2010 in Phoenix. This was not an easy decision to make, although the venue had been scheduled several years before the passage of SB 1070. A boycott was briefly considered, although both our Presiding Bishop Katharine Jefferts Schori and I strongly advocated keeping the meeting in Phoenix as a way to learn more about immigration on the frontlines as well as to support those who were most economically affected by the boycott—hotel workers and those low-paid workers dependent on the tourist industry. When the green light for the Phoenix location was finally given, I decided that it would helpful to have a preconvention trip to the border, so that bishops who so wished could have the experience of crossing into Mexico and meeting those most affected. I knew that they could not fail to be as moved as I had been in 2004. We named the trip "Bishops on the Border."

It wasn't easy getting more than thirty bishops from all over the country to a remote site on the Arizona/Mexico border, but with help from border missioner, the Rev. Seth Poley, and his committee, we managed to coordinate flights into Sky Harbor Airport and get everyone and their luggage on a bus on September 13, 2010. I was especially grateful that the Presiding Bishop of the Episcopal Church had enthusiastically taken time from her hectic schedule to travel with us. During the five-hour trip to our hotel in Douglas, Arizona, we were given an orientation by the

Rev. Debbie Noonan, a recent seminary graduate and bilingual assistant priest at Trinity Cathedral in Phoenix. Thanks to an onboard video system, we were able to watch the film *800 Mile Wall* (www.800milewall.org). With its graphic pictures of corpses recovered from the desert, it left us with disturbing visual images of the issues we would soon hear about. Looking out the bus window, we experienced the majesty of the southern Arizona desert in a summer thunderstorm. Internally, we prepared for the ugliness of human injustice and oppression, and the despair of grinding poverty.

Early the next day we divided into several smaller groups to travel in vans to various destinations. Some crossed over in the border town of Aqua Prieta, Sonora, opposite Douglas, Arizona. Others, including my group, headed for the smaller town of Naco, Sonora. In both places we were able to visit shelters for those who had made it through the fence and headed north, only to be caught by the Border Patrol agents and sent back. In many cases those "deported" had lost everything except the clothes on their backs. My group was able to have a long conversation through a translator with one young man who had attempted to cross with his family, been caught, and sent back to Naco. He was close to tears as he described their uncertain future. They were literally caught between two worlds, with no job, no family support, and no money to get home to southern Mexico. He would have to do his best to scrape together enough money to make another attempt at the dangerous crossing.

The news we heard was not all bad. Various church groups and nonprofit agencies have been laboring to ease the situation of immigrants caught between two countries. We had the chance to visit a medical clinic, a feeding program, and a twelve-step shelter for those afflicted with alcohol and/or drug addiction. This was where I had previously witnessed the wonderful work of a community called CREEDA, located in Aqua Prieta, in sight of the border fence. There is no state-sponsored program for addicts or the mentally ill in this region of Mexico, so this private group does its best to care for patients who are literally dropped at their doorstep by the local police. Run by former addict Juan Garcia, he credits the program for saving his life. After getting clean and sober, he stayed on as director, doing his best to care for about eighty clients from twelve to eighty years old, all squeezed into a ramshackle but well-maintained compound. At the center of the structure is an enclosed patio for the most profoundly mentally ill. "These are my angels," Juan said softly. "God put me here to serve them, and I won't leave them no matter what."

That evening we regrouped in Douglas for a panel presentation given by local people presenting various sides of the issue. On the stage were a local rancher, a community activist, an emergency room doctor, the local police chief, and a senior official from the Border Patrol. Each spoke passionately and movingly about their experiences, and, of course, each had a different idea as to how the problem might be solved. But what they had in common was a deep-seated frustration that almost verged upon despair. The rancher spoke of how his land was being trashed and how his supply of ranch hands and workers had disappeared. The doctor spoke of the difficulty and expense of transferring injured immigrants from the desert to hospital facilities in Tucson. The local police chief talked of battling a rising crime rate with limited resources, while the Border Patrol officer shared his frustration at being labeled a sadistic storm trooper by the political left, or as an incompetent bureaucrat by the extreme right. "We are just doing our best to enforce the law of the land, whether we like that law or not," he explained. We all left the meeting with a deeper awareness that there is no easy solution to this issue, but that we in the church can play a valuable role in simply being a safe place where all can come together.

Perhaps the most memorable event of our time together came just before the panel presentation when we participated in a vigil that is held weekly at the border checkpoint. Every Thursday evening a handful of local residents, both Hispanic and Anglo, and representing several churches, gather alongside the main highway leading into Mexico. Each holds aloft a small white cross bearing the name of a person who has died in the desert and the date their body was recovered. Each marcher in turn holds up their cross, loudly calls out the name of the person written on it, to which the other marchers shout *"Presente!"* Many of these crosses have no name, simply a date and the words, *"No identificado."* A photo of thirty-five bishops in their purple shirts holding white crosses was the image that appeared in the local Arizona papers. But more important, it was an image that will ever remain in our hearts. The Rev. Mark Adams, organizer of the event and contributor to this book, presented us all with one of these crosses to take back home. I know many of those bishops take their crosses with them on visitations in their dioceses, speak about their experience on the border, and witness to a wider national audience the plight of those who continue to die in the desert.

The last year or so has been a time of increasing involvement in the immigration struggle both for Episcopalians and for our fellow Christians in Arizona. It has also been the issue for which I receive more critical public reaction than on any other position I take. I am glad to say that most of those attacks have come from non-Episcopalians who write to me complaining that I am un-American, or that I advocate harboring criminals. Still, I am very much aware that many in my flock disagree with me, and in a handful of cases parishioners have left their local church because of what I have written or said. On the positive side, I have been gratified by the support from my colleagues in other churches. More broadly, the Rev. Jan Flaaten, recently retired president of the Arizona Ecumenical Council, has coordinated efforts among many denominations. The lay-people and clergy of the East Valley Interfaith movement have been a tremendous resource. There is never a public meeting dealing with humane immigration reform at which some Arizona clergy are not represented. Most gratifying of all has been the fellowship developed with the bishops in the Roman Catholic, United Methodist, and Lutheran churches. I am in awe of their faithful advocacy for the rights of all God's people. This book is just one small example of our collaboration.

It has been nearly eight years now since I first rode that bus across the border to meet firsthand the men, women, and children who are risking everything for the chance of a better life in this country. At the time, I had no idea that their stories would become so much a part of mine, their physical journey so much a part of my faith journey. What they have done for me in their suffering, in their patience, and in their hope, is far more than anything I can ever do for them.

Not long ago I was interviewed for a Public Television show on immigration. Toward the end of the discussion, the interviewer turned to me and asked, "So, Bishop, what are we going to do with these people?" The answer came to my lips faster than I could choose my words, "These are not 'those people'" I said, "They are my people, they are our country's people, and they are God's people." That is what being a bishop on the border has taught me.

As this little book goes to press, there are some hopeful signs. We can pray that both local and national leaders will recognize that what we face is the greatest human rights challenge of our time, and put aside their political differences in favor of humanitarian solutions. We can pray that those of us who call ourselves Christians will not turn our backs on our brothers and sisters in need, and that we will never forget *"Dios no tiene fronteras*—God has no borders."

4 | We are All Cousins

A Biblical Mandate

Stephen Talmage

I am a native of the southwest United States and for fifty of my fifty-four years I have lived either in Tucson, Arizona, or the metro Phoenix area. Since being elected in June 2006 to serve as bishop of the Grand Canyon Synod (Arizona and Southern Nevada) of the Evangelical Lutheran Church in America, I have been urged, invited, and convicted to engage in the complex drama of immigration facing our nation and the territory to which I have been called. As a spiritual leader who is often asked to speak before diverse assemblies, I want to appreciate the variety of perspectives that individuals and communities represent. As a Christian leader, my main frame of reference is always going to be Christ and the witness of scripture. So my primary motivation for engagement and advocacy around the issue of SB

1070 and the need for comprehensive immigration reform come from the reading of God's continuous story of deliverance, of compassion, of reconciliation, and of radical hospitality. As a student of the Bible, one cannot escape the clear mandate of Hebrew Scripture that blocking the stranger or mistreating the alien among us was failing to live out the identity to which God's people had been called. As God often declared, "Remember, Israel, you were once aliens." Or read through the four gospel accounts of the life and ministry of Jesus. One cannot help but notice that Jesus was very intentional about crossing barriers and overcoming obstacles to create access and availability to God's unconditional love for and forgiveness to the least, the last, the lost, and the little.

When one considers God's call to welcome the stranger, to serve the oppressed, and to accompany the unfortunate in our midst, the Old Testament witness that best accompanies such actions is the story of the exodus. Out of compassion, God, in God's timing, responds to the painful cries of Israel after they have been suffering under the tyranny and brutality of the Pharaoh. The exodus event was a faith-shaping and life-defining experience. That experience provided the identifying mark of knowing and remembering what it is like to live under oppression and in bondage to slavery, as well as what is like to be set free.

Enjoining others in conversation around SB 1070 and the challenge of the immigrant today is to remind myself and those in the conversation that unless we are a descendent of one of the few indigenous tribes of Arizona, we are all immigrants. In order to maintain a spirit of humility in what often becomes a platform for self-righteousness and nativist arrogance, remembering that either one or most of one's ancestors came here from somewhere else is critical to the conversation. As people of faith, who have the witness of Scripture: God is intentional about forming a community of people, whom God seeks to bless, but with the expectation that they, in turn, will be a blessing to the families of the earth (Genesis 12:3).

Continuing to place ourselves within the exodus event, persons of faith are called to remember their immigrant status, allowing that recognition to shape individual or communal responses to the stranger or alien:

> For the LORD your God is God of gods and Lord of lords, the great God, mighty and awesome, who is not partial and takes no bribe, who executes justice for the orphan and the widow, and who loves the strangers, providing them with food and clothing. You shall also love the stranger, for you were strangers in the land of Egypt. (Deuteronomy 10:17–19)
>
> You shall not wrong or oppress a resident alien, for you were aliens in the land of Egypt. You shall not abuse any widow or orphan. (Exodus 22:21–22)
>
> When an alien resides with you in your land, you shall not oppress the alien. The alien who resides with you shall be to you as the citizen among you; you shall love the alien as yourself, for you were aliens in the land of Egypt: I am the LORD your God. (Leviticus 19:33–34)

These passages, along with many more, affirm over and over again the attitude and the hospitality that are to be expressed to the alien and the stranger living among us. As fellow Lutherans Stephen Bouman and Ralston Deffenbaugh write in *They Are Us: Lutherans and Immigration*, "Caring for the alien, the stranger, the oppressed is not an option for people of the Jewish or Christian faith—it is God's will. The plight of the dispossessed matters to God. It must matter to God's people."[1]

---

1   Stephen Bouman and Ralston Deffenbaugh, *They Are Us: Lutherans and Immigration* (Minneapolis: Augsburg Fortress, 2009), 11.

One of the great mission texts in the Old Testament is that sung by the psalmist:

> Happy are those whose help is the God of Jacob,
> whose hope is in the LORD their God,
> who executes justice for the oppressed;
> who gives food to the hungry.
> The LORD sets the prisoners free;
> the LORD opens the eyes of the blind.
> The LORD lifts up those who are bowed down;
> the LORD loves the righteous.
> The LORD watches over the strangers;
> he upholds the orphan and the widow,
> but the way of the wicked he brings to ruin.
> (Psalm 146:5, 7–9)

Though the Old Testament narrative is filled with stories of human beings struggling to live out God's intent for humanity, another thread is through the narrative: God desires to work through God's people to present a new reality. Though God's people struggle with the responsibility of receiving the blessing of God for the sake of being a blessing to others, this does not change God's intent. The prophets of God continued to cry out to God's people to turn from their idolatry, their immorality, their injustice, their ungratefulness, and their practice of empty rituals. They proclaimed a vision that reflects the words of the song of Psalm 146.

This vision does not change with the arrival of Jesus. Several years ago I sat with colleague bishops of the ELCA in the sanctuary of Luther Memorial Church in Washington, D.C. Our guest preacher for the day was Jim Wallis, the founder and executive director of Sojourners. Sojourners was founded in 1971 with a mission to articulate the biblical call to social justice, inspiring hope and building a movement to transform individuals, communities, the church, and the world. The text for his sermon that day was Luke 4:16–21:

> When he came to Nazareth, where he had been brought up, he went to the synagogue on the sabbath day, as was his custom. He stood up to read, and the scroll of the prophet Isaiah was given to him. He unrolled the scroll and found the place where it was written:
> "The Spirit of the Lord is upon me,
> because he has anointed me
> to bring good news to the poor.
> He has sent me to proclaim release to the captives
> and recovery of sight to the blind,
> to let the oppressed go free,
> to proclaim the year of the Lord's favor."
> And he rolled up the scroll, gave it back to the attendant, and sat down. The eyes of all in the synagogue were fixed on him. Then he began to say to them, "Today this scripture has been fulfilled in your hearing."

Fresh from his baptism in the Jordan River and his time facing the devil and temptation in the desert, Jesus goes to his hometown synagogue and he is invited to offer the message for the day. He reads these words from Isaiah and just about creates a riot. His audience thinks he is practicing blasphemy or claiming the attributes of God when, in their eyes, he is just the son of a local carpenter. However, in the context of Luke's gospel, Jesus is setting the foundation for the work he came to accomplish. What Jim Wallis emphasized that day is that this sermon comes at the beginning of Jesus's public ministry. Wallis went on to say, "I believe this is Jesus's mission statement." And then he asked, "And how many of our congregations have a similar mission?"

Once again Bouman and Deffenbaugh write, "Jesus' story as recorded in the four Gospels, is the story of welcome, of inclusion, of hospitality, of service to both Jew and Gentile, to citizens of Israel and to the strangers in their midst, particularly those who were considered outsiders, unclean and not worthy of human dignity."[2]

One of the great attributes of Jesus was his ability to tell stories or parables that used everyday elements, but contained one clear spiritual insight or challenge. One of his more famous parables is that of the Good Samaritan, found in Luke 10. The context for this story and many of Jesus's stories is that religiously right-thinking, rule-following, and highly educated leaders are seeking to test, trap, or trick Jesus into saying something they can use to discredit his feared influence and popularity. In the case of the Good Samaritan, the questioner is a lawyer inquiring what he must do to inherit eternal life. Jesus, being a good rabbi, answers one question with two questions, "What is written in the law? What do you read there?" The lawyer responds with what has been called the Great Commandment, "You shall love the Lord your God with all your heart, and with all your soul, and with all your strength, and with all of your mind; and your neighbor as yourself." Jesus affirms his answer. But the lawyer is not satisfied. He wants to see if he can still catch Jesus slipping up and possibly incriminating himself. Luke indicates the lawyer wants to justify himself, so he asks Jesus another question, "And who is my neighbor?"

This is an important question in seeking to live faithfully along the border. This is an important question for all followers of Jesus. It is simple to define neighbor as the person in proximity next to where I live, work, or play. But in light of the parable how are we to answer that question?

---

2 Bouman and Deffenbaugh, *They Are Us*, 13.

The story from Jesus may help us:

> Jesus replied, "A man was going down from Jerusalem to Jericho, and fell into the hands of robbers, who stripped him, beat him, and went away, leaving him half dead. Now by chance a priest was going down that road; and when he saw him, he passed by on the other side. So likewise a Levite, when he came to the place and saw him, passed by on the other side. But a Samaritan while travelling came near him; and when he saw him, he was moved with pity. He went to him and bandaged his wounds, having poured oil and wine on them. Then he put him on his own animal, brought him to an inn, and took care of him. The next day he took out two denarii, gave them to the innkeeper, and said, 'Take care of him; and when I come back, I will repay you whatever more you spend.' Which of these three, do you think, was a neighbor to the man who fell into the hands of the robbers?" He said, "The one who showed him mercy." Jesus said to him, "Go and do likewise." (Luke 10:30–37)

As we engage in conversation about difficult and emotional issues, a familiar litany is framed with the words, "Yes, but." When Jesus says, "Go and do likewise," I have heard the following, "Yes, but does that include people who have entered our country illegally?" My response is to ask what it really means to love one's neighbor like oneself even if that neighbor is undocumented. Do we continue to tolerate an immigration system that divides and destroys family unity? Do we continue to tolerate legal and economic systems that ignore human rights and open the door to exploitation of workers? Do we continue to tolerate an immigration system that has not really worked for forty-plus years and actually encourages the 11 to 12 million undocumented residents in this country to live in the shadows of our community, plagued by a cloud of fear? Do we continue to tolerate an immigration system that is anything but efficient, even when individuals seek to follow all the rules? Do we continue to tolerate an immigration system that offers no means by which individuals (some who have lived in, worked in, and paid taxes to this country for twenty to thirty years) can secure permanent resident status without being deported and excluded for a minimum of ten years? Do we continue to tolerate an immigration system that does not address the mixed message we continue to communicate because of our own economic or security interests, boldly declaring, "No Trespassing," while seeking "Help Wanted"? How is a neighbor to respond to his or her neighbor in light of both the witness of the Hebrew Scriptures and Jesus?

A while back, conservative commentator Glenn Beck issued a strong warning to his disciples that they should avoid being a part of any church where social justice is proclaimed. The issue of social justice cannot be avoided when addressing immigration in this country. As a preacher and a teacher who affirms that the scriptures are authoritative and set the norm for one's understanding of the Christian faith, it seems to me that part of the resistance to Christ and his followers was the social, cultural, and national barriers that Jesus commanded to be crossed. At the end of the Gospel according to Matthew, Jesus offers a bookend to the Great Commandment to love God and to love one's neighbor as oneself. We get what has been called the Great Commission:

> And Jesus came and said to them, "All authority in heaven and on earth has been given to me. Go therefore and make disciples of all nations, baptizing them in the name of the Father and of the Son and of the Holy Spirit, and teaching them to obey everything that I have commanded you. And

remember, I am with you always, to the end of the age." (Matthew 28:18–20)

Immediately before his ascension into heaven, Jesus instructs his disciples to go back to Jerusalem and wait for the gift and the power of the Holy Spirit. This instruction will take them out of the familiar and into new territories and relationships. For such transformation to happen there is an affirmation of the need of the Holy Spirit to empower the followers of Jesus:

> "But you will receive power when the Holy Spirit has come upon you; and you will be my witnesses in Jerusalem, in all Judea and Samaria, and to the ends of the earth." (Acts 1:8)

The message and the mission of Jesus Christ as witnessed in the four gospels transcended lines and boundaries. This was radical. It was countercultural. It threatened the status quo. It eliminated any sense that one group had the upper hand on anyone else.

The impact of this witness and the movement of the Holy Spirit became evident when Saul, former zealous persecutor of the Christian faith, now converted and called Paul, writes about the challenges facing the Christian community in Galatia. Paul gives voice to the transnational identity of the faith community:

> As many of you as were baptized into Christ have clothed yourselves with Christ. There is no longer Jew or Greek, there is no longer slave or free, there is no longer male and female; for all of you are one in Christ Jesus. (Galatians 3:27–28)

Through baptism and incorporation in Christ, one discovers a capacity to cross boundaries and to live with new loyalties.

From the witness of scripture, the lines are not always neat and clean. There is a lot of gray and ambiguity in what it means to practice radical hospitality, particularly when we know from the witness of Jesus and the early church that the love of God offered in Jesus has no conditions. Where there appears clarity is that in the face of human suffering or injustice imposed upon or practiced toward another human being, the people of God are not to be silent, passive, or apathetic. The call to practice respect, compassion, and mercy allows this world to see a God of love and justice with skin on. The work of advocacy, particularly for those with no voice, or a limited one, in the public square, is not some liberal, progressive, political movement of the church; it appears to be a core ingredient of what it means to be the church.

Personal Connection

Everyone has a story of migration, if they are open to look at their family history. Some of my ancestors came across the Atlantic in the early days of colonial immigration and occupation, some in the mid-nineteenth century. They hailed from Scotland, Wales, and England. They sought out new opportunities, primarily economic opportunities, considering it worth the risk and expense to improve their lot with the promise America held. From the Eastern shores, branches of my family tree ventured to the Midwest, West, and South. Connection with our nation's border with Mexico came when my father's maternal grandfather relocated to the Southwest. Dr. William Pickles was a young company doctor with a wife and daughter. He worked for a mining company in the appropriately named town of Coal City, Illinois. Practicing medicine shortly after the turn of the twentieth century exposed him to the assortment of popular and challenging ailments. Due to the lack of advancement in medical treatment options and antibiotics, measles, polio, scarlet fever, pneumonia, and tuberculosis shortened lives and threatened whole communities. Unfortunately, he was not immune and contracted tuberculosis. Other medical colleagues advised him to practice the standard treatment of the day and move to a drier climate for rest. In 1906, the decision was made to relocate to El Paso, Texas. I don't know if my great-grandfather really knew much about Texas or the border town of El Paso. I don't know if he was aware that right across the Rio Grande River a civil war was about to break out between the soldiers of President Diaz and the revolutionary opponents being led by Pancho Villa and other opposition leaders. What I am sure he did know was that the climate of El Paso offered a person with TB the chance to fight off the infection and find restoration of one's body.

Because of the current push among some politicians and law enforcement officials to secure the border with more invincible measures, it is difficult for many to comprehend what life along the border was like one hundred years ago. When my great-grandfather, great-grandmother, and grandmother arrived in El Paso, the community operated with an open border. Workers and commerce flowed freely across the Santa Fe Bridge that connected El Paso to Ciudad Juarez. The local smelter, a cigar factory, a cement plant, and construction projects required large numbers of workers from both sides of the border. One only needs to remember that it was a little over sixty years earlier that El Paso was annexed into the United States through the Treaty of Guadalupe Hildalgo; it would not be unusual to find residents of El Paso with extended family relationships in Ciudad Juarez or other Mexican villages across the border. Given that Ciudad Juarez has always been larger than El Paso, cooperative and collaborative relationships were critical for both communities to prosper.

Consider the example of Chihuahuita:

Chihuahuita, El Paso's smallest and oldest neighborhood, has played an important part in the city's development for more than four hundred years. There were scattered Manso Indian settlements in the late sixteenth century and the area became an important part of the farming and irrigation system developed by the Spaniards. In 1818, Ricardo Brusuelas received a land grant from the Spanish and established a ranch here, irrigating his land from the nearby "acequia de Chamizal." Although lightly populated, this area was the site of a popular ford on the Rio Grande, frequented by travelers on the Camino Real and Chihuahua Trail. Although the Treaty of Guadalupe Hidalgo made the river the international boundary between Mexico and the United States, placing Chihuahuita in American El Paso, the essential character of the area changed little. As many of the settlers came from across the river in the state of Chihuahua, the area became known as Chihuahuita or "little Chihuahua."

Chihuahuita grew with the arrival of the Santa Fe Railroad in 1881. It became a crowded urban neighborhood and was designated the First Ward of El Paso in 1887. The railroad and businesses such as the El Paso Laundry Company on Seventh Street brought jobs to the area. The wooden Santa Fe Bridge was constructed, connecting Chihuahuita with Ciudad Juarez and becoming the main entryway for goods and people into El Paso.

The Mexican Revolution of 1910 brought a surge of refugees north, many to Chihuahuita. The area swarmed with new arrivals, became a center of revolutionary intrigue, and offered good views of the fighting across the river. Historical records indicate that both President Diaz and Pancho Villa crossed the river and held strategic planning meetings.[3]

It was the setting for a story that has influenced my understanding of being a faithful leader living along the border. Though making the move to El Paso to save his own health,

---

3 Research Packet and Narrative by: Fred Morales, Jamie Carter, Dr. George D. Torok, Honors Project Spring 2002, National Endowment for the Humanities Historical Markers Project, Chihuahuita.

my great-grandfather could not abandon the calling God had placed on him to be a healer. Upon graduating from Rush Medical School, my great-grandfather took an oath, the Hippocratic Oath, which states, "I will treat without exception all who seek my ministrations. . . ." The flow of human need, as my great-grandfather sought to rebuild his strength, was too much to ignore. When it became known that my great-grandfather was a medical doctor, requests came for help. The volume of requests forced him to limit his practice to surgery. In faithfulness to the oath he took, my great-grandfather willed his body to tend to the physical needs of the community. He neither asked for immigration papers, nor did he require his patients to speak English first. Again and again, he was called upon to cross the border into Juarez to treat the wounded. When wounded or sick soldiers were brought to his care, he did not show preference to one side or another. He simply tended with compassion and faithfulness to a promise he made when he became a doctor. This act of service and commitment did not come without personal cost. My great-grandfather, who had regained much strength with the move to El Paso, relapsed with the burden of broken bodies begging for his skills. He died in his early forties in 1916. In 1918, under- standing the importance of education, my grandmother was accepted into college at the University of Arizona in Tucson. Tucson sits just sixty miles north of the border between the United States and Mexico. It was in Tucson that I was born and raised, a little over one hundred years after the Gadsen Purchase. In 1853, in an effort to secure territory to provide a southern railroad connection to the Pacific, American president Franklin Pierce utilized the negotiation skills of his minister to Mexico, James Gadsen, to purchase thirty thousand square miles of land that ran from El Paso, Texas, to the Southern California coast. Much like in El Paso, the movement of people between the two countries was seen as a given rather than a threat. From the mid-1800s until the mid-1920s, workers flowed back and forth from Mexico to the United States without need for visas or other documentation. The relationship between the two countries around the turn of the century was symbiotic; U.S. railroad companies, mines, and ranches needed labor, and Mexicans needed jobs. Although not an official policy, this is considered by some researchers as the first bracero, or guest worker program for Mexicans. Unemployed Mexican workers found jobs in border regions, and American companies found workers who could be hired at lower than normal wages. Subsequent guest worker programs (official and unofficial) were to follow. During World War I, Mexican laborers were recruited through mass media and word of mouth to fill jobs left vacant by active servicemen. Their labor helped to contribute to a growing, robust domestic economy, as U.S. businesses profited from the lower wages paid to Mexican workers.[4]

This flow of workers, and even the attitude toward the immigrant, was always shaped by the economic need and political climate in the United States. In 1924, Congress passed the Johnson-Reed Act. This immigration law created quotas, new visa requirements, and controls on the border. In the opinion of some, this legislation was a move to address the increasing number of Chinese workers coming into the country as well as the fear of importing the rising and competing ideology of communism. It allowed for the forced deportation of those who did not meet the requirements. But the demand for low-cost agricultural and other workers continued to inspire employers to find creative ways to meet the needs of the marketplace when the home-grown labor pool was depleted by men and women called into military service or the expansion of the American economy. The Bracero (literally, one who works with his arms)

---

4   "Looking Back: The History of U.S. (Im)migration," centerwest.org/wp-content/uploads/2011/01/eastman2008.

Program was a series of laws and agreements developed with Mexico in response to the need for more workers to support the demands of the marketplace. It ran from 1942–1964. The premise of this action was to create a steady pool of manual laborers, particularly for the United States agri-business. It created legal residency for the laborers during a time of need and employment and then required workers to return to Mexico when the work was completed. In addition, this program allowed much better tracking of who was coming and going across the border. A downside to this program was that, rather than control the immigration of both legal and undocumented workers, it actually increased the number of undocumented workers coming to America. Because the Bracero Program as it evolved agreed to pay a minimum wage, provide housing and other benefits, the economic incentive, in light of earnings potential in Mexico, motivated many to continue to seek to cross the border illegally.

Because of the historic flow of Mexican residents in and out of Arizona, as well as longtime Mexican residents whose nationality was changed by a line and contract made between the United States and Mexico in 1853, I was raised with neighbors who were Mexican-American, or in some cases Mexican. The classrooms in which I was a student and the sports teams on which I played were integrated; the issue of ethnicity did not seem to matter. But the world in which we live has gone through some great changes, and the challenge of immigration is one of those. Because the current immigration system has been ineffective for a very long time and the desire for many who want to come into this country exceeds the capacity of the current system, attempts to change laws, control the numbers, and restrict access have dominated the debate of most recent times. Underlying the variety of rhetoric on immigration is the fact that after the attacks of September 11, 2001, the worldview for many in this country changed from one of optimism to one of fear. This fear has pushed our country to expand law enforcement and security along our borders in significant ways. Though debated, depending on which side of the argument you find yourself, recent Border Patrol efforts, expansion of barriers along the border, increased use of technology, the passing of SB 1070, and the Great Recession have lowered the number of people making their way north of the U.S./Mexico border. But still the desire to feed families back home, to reunite with families in the United States, to secure a livable wage, or to escape oppression in their native land fuels individuals to take even riskier measures to make their way into our country.

Personal Context

In this synod of the ELCA, we have a very small congregation in Douglas in southeast Arizona and two congregations in Yuma in the southwest corner of Arizona. In the metro Phoenix area, we have three specifically Latino mission outposts and three Anglo congregations who have developed an outreach to their Latino neighbors, as well as one Latino mission in Tucson. They all have stories linked to the immigration history of the Southwest as well as the personal and communal challenges the current immigration system presents. The three congregations situated along the Arizona/Mexico border are Anglo congregations. Immanuel Lutheran Church in Douglas has been a base for Lutheran and other Christian groups to travel across the border into the city of Agua Prieta. These groups participate in constructing basic adobe, wood, and metal houses to replace the patchwork of discarded lumber, tarps, and doors that serve as residences for many. Faith Lutheran Church is the oldest ELCA congregation in Yuma. Out of this ministry, American Beginnings was developed in 1988 as a family and social services outreach, with a particular emphasis of providing support for immigrants to become naturalized citizens. Gloria de Cristo Lutheran Church developed in the foothills area of Yuma; its membership is primarily snowbird residents from the North and Upper Midwest.

As leaders within these communities engage the issue of immigration reform, one would expect to hear diverse viewpoints. Within the Anglo congregations, one would hear a sense of compassion, frustration with the current system, as well as concerns for how undocumented residents put a drain on health, education, and medical resources, or influence local criminal activity. It is not unusual to hear division of opinion over the desire for the cheap labor the immigrants provide both personally or in the community, as well as how they are perceived to be driving wages down and taking jobs away from legal residents. When one lives so close to the border, with the increasing violence due to drug cartels and the smuggling of arms, human beings, and drugs, there is strong support to secure the border, and much of this gets additional support from Anglos further away from the border.

Within the Latino communities, the overwhelming difficulty is the reality of or fear of deportation, loss of income, separation from family members who are legal residents or citizens, and the increasing experience of racial profiling. The impact of SB 1070 on individuals and local Latino faith communities within the Grand Canyon Synod cannot be overestimated. Each ministry has experienced what some would say is the goal of the law: an out migration of individuals and families either to other places in the United States or back to Mexico. It is the voices of children that concern me most, as they are either U.S. citizens or were brought to this country at a young age. They are immersed in American culture, they speak English, but they are terrified that when they come home from school their mother or father may have been snatched away, put into detention, and sent back to Mexico, and it may be years before they will see them again. They also know the high cost and dangers of attempting to recross the border, as current enforcement has moved those seeking to enter the United States to contract with human-smuggling syndicates, known as coyotes, and the migration paths have moved to more dangerous and harsher portions of the expansive southern Arizona border.

This is what one of the Anglo leaders from the Yuma area shared with me:

> The Organ Pipe Cactus National Monument is pretty dangerous because of the drug and immigrant smuggling that uses that area as a route of passage. The Border Patrol is constantly making busts for meth, cocaine, or marijuana. From time to time, a drug house in Yuma is seized. Automobile insurance is higher here because of the number of cars that are stolen and go over the border before authorities know about the theft.

From another Anglo leader in Yuma:

> People are still told in Mexico that all they need to do if they have a need for heart or joint surgery is simply to get to Yuma Regional Medical Center. YRMC is reported to be the most expensive hospital in the state because of the border loss. This is unfair and unjust. My thought is that those who advocate open borders should pay for it—but unfortunately, we all pay.

Prior to President Obama's directive to U.S. Immigration and Customs Enforcement to focus attention only on individuals suspected of criminal behavior, repeat border-crossers, and recent border-crossers, one of our Latino leaders offered a different perspective of life in our Latino communities under the cloud of SB 1070:

> Sadly, I have another story for you. A woman who used to go to Pan de Vida had moved to Goodyear with her new common-law husband. Within the last couple of days, they were stopped while driving, for no apparent reason. The officer immediately asked them for Social Security cards, etc. The woman protested the new law wasn't yet in effect, but the officer insisted anyway. Unable to produce the documents, the cop called ICE. Apparently they weren't going to come, so the cop drove the couple to an immigration office and turned them over. The woman was released and has a court date pending. The man just signed his voluntary return to Mexico. Two of the woman's four sons are U.S citizens.
>
> The woman doesn't have enough money for an attorney, so she and her compadres asked if they could hold a yard sale in the Pan de Vida parking lot to help raise some funds. Obviously, I said yes. Whoever tells you there will be no racial profiling is not telling the truth. Whoever says stops will only be made and papers asked for in the course of investigating a crime is also not being truthful. Overzealous officers will find whatever pretext to justify a stop but the fact seems to be that people will be stopped for Driving While Mexican . . . and SB 1070 isn't yet even in effect!

Or another story:

> A recurrent theme also emerged in our prayers yesterday and I was asked to bring it to you and the synod, hoping you could also take it to the

appropriate channels at the ELCA regarding immigration reform.

The latest manifestation of our community's
pain over this issue was the arrest by MCSO (Maricopa County Sheriff's Office) deputies of Hector
Aguirre. Hector has no papers, but his wife, Olga,
and the kids are U.S. citizens. Hector is the family
provider, although Olga works some. She is a
kidney transplant survivor and still has to have
dialysis, takes tons of meds, and still ends up hospitalized from time to time. In fact, she just got
out of the hospital.

Like in many families in the ELCA, there has
been less or no work for our families. For many
of our families, there really wasn't ever any abun-
dance anyway, but now it is worse. For families like
the Aguirre's, the likely deportation of the father
and breadwinner is a severe blow. It hurts that
family, but it also hurts our congregation and our
community at large.

Nobody is asking for handouts—simply the
opportunity to work and live like anyone else. Comprehensive immigration reform is badly needed.

The plea yesterday was that the ELCA speak up
yet again and loudly, using whatever influence possible to help bring change about. There are many
other issues on the ELCA's plate and some, like
the gay issue, may seem more pressing as people
are already leaving the ELCA. I think everyone
realizes our concern is not the only one of importance, but it is important. The problem now is
literally destroying families.

When the U.S. Supreme Court ruled on SB 1070 on June 25,
2012, I was invited to share what the impact has been since

the law was first passed by the State of Arizona Legislature and signed by Governor Jan Brewer.

The recent decision of the Supreme Court to uphold most pieces of Arizona Senate Bill 1070 has created a different response than when it first was signed by Governor Jan Brewer. Leading up to and after the signing, combined with the collapse of the construction industry and loss of significant jobs, there was a demonstrable exodus of undocumented persons. It is estimated of the 450,000 undocumented persons living in the state of Arizona at that time, close to 200,000 left the state from the end of 2008 to the beginning of 2010. As has been attested in our congregations ministering with Latinos, many in those communities live under a cloud of fear. The loss of job opportunities, the political climate, and inconsistent practice among various law enforcement agencies have deeply reinforced a message that Arizona is not the place to come. Since the Supreme Court's ruling last week, the migration out has stopped. The Mexican Consulate in Phoenix previously was inundated with requests for papers to travel back to Mexico. Now there is a normal pattern of requests for powers of attorney by parents to protect their children in the event that they might be arrested, but in light of the president's executive actions and even the Department of Homeland Security's practice, there is not an overriding fear of deportation, but a recognition that one might be arrested without proper paperwork. Most undocumented immigrants are taking a "wait and see" attitude in light of the law's effect being dependent on a lower court's lifting of the stay on the "papers please" provision and no one knows when that will be. The Department of Homeland Security has directed immigration officials in Arizona not to deport undocumented persons identified through enforcement of SB 1070 unless they meet the agency's priorities of being dangerous criminals, recent border crossers, or repeat immigration violators. Of course, among some elected state officials, there are calls for the state to enforce current laws and protect its border, viewing the federal government as failing in that task, while others continue to raise the caution flag for the potential of racial profiling. All sides continue to plead for the Congress to enact comprehensive immigration reform.

At our recent Grand Canyon Synod Assembly (May 30 through June 1, 2012) in Las Vegas, a majority of voting members passed the following resolution:

WHEREAS, the stated purpose of this Synod, its congregations, and its ministry organizations, is grounded in the love of neighbor as Jesus commanded, and includes "advocating dignity and justice for all people" and "standing with the poor and powerless," both within the church and society (S6, C4); and

WHEREAS, the 2012 Assembly of the Grand Canyon Synod of the Evangelical Lutheran Church in America is collectively engaging the theme of "Welcoming Justice," and is carefully considering how matters of hospitality are linked to matters of social justice; and

WHEREAS, the Church Council of the Evangelical Lutheran Church in America has adopted considerate and informed statements on immigration in 1998 ("Immigration") and 2009 ("Toward

Compassionate, Just, and Wise Immigration Reform") which clearly articulate fundamental realities and challenges of race, law, fairness, theology, and economics; and

WHEREAS, some congregations and clergy in this synod have borne witness to increased discrimination and harassment of their members and worshipers since the signing of Arizona SB 1070 ("Support Our Law Enforcement and Safe Neighborhoods Act") in the spring of 2010; and

WHEREAS, some among us object to Arizona's immigration law on moral and humanitarian grounds, others among us object on principles of civil rights and race, and still others object due to economic concerns;

BE IT THEREFORE RESOLVED, the Grand Canyon Synod of the Evangelical Lutheran Church in America, meeting in assembly, exhorts the members of its congregations to treat all human beings, regardless of immigration status, as creatures made in the image of God, possessing dignity, worth, and value conferred by their Creator; and

BE IT FURTHER RESOLVED, the Grand Canyon Synod of the Evangelical Lutheran Church in America, meeting in assembly, concludes that Arizona SB 1070 is inconsistent with our collective Christian belief and witness, and harmful to the practical concerns and needs of Arizona; and

BE IT FURTHER RESOLVED, the Grand Canyon Synod of the Evangelical Lutheran Church in America, meeting in assembly, concludes that immigration is of significant importance to our members and congregations in Nevada and Utah, as well as those in Arizona; that Arizona's SB 1070 is before the Supreme Court and may be deemed a matter of federal law; and therefore this Synod exhorts its members and congregations in all states to encourage their leaders in the federal government to work for bipartisan immigration reform that is comprehensive, fair, humane, compassionate, and which safeguards the unity of families; and

BE IT FURTHER RESOLVED, the Grand Canyon Synod of the Evangelical Lutheran Church in America, meeting in assembly, instructs the Secretary of this Synod to address and forward this resolution to the Office of the Governor of the State of Arizona, the President of the Arizona State Senate, and the Speaker of the Arizona State House of Representatives, with individual copies sent to all members of the Arizona Legislature.

My office has had only a couple of elected officials respond back when we have sent them this resolution. The debate will continue. The impact is unknown. Our synod and our state are still deeply divided on the issue. But it is hoped that recent actions can be an impetus for mobilizing leaders on both sides to work together to resolve a decades' long failure of our federal government to address a major issue that impacts communities, congregations, and families.

Within these little vignettes, one can read the dilemma facing our churches and our country. To some in the faith community I serve and beyond, the broken immigration system is perceived as a threat, a burden, and an economic liability. To others, the broken immigration system means having no means to find a path toward legal residency and the opportunity to keep a family intact, as well as constantly living in fear of being profiled because of one's appearance or accent.

A Lutheran Response

Immigration issues are complex. As Lutherans, we approach the issues facing us from the perspective of what Martin Luther called living in two kingdoms: the kingdom on the left and the kingdom on the right. The left is the realm of civil law. Lutherans understand the need to struggle with others to develop proposals, resolutions, and even laws that serve not just individual or national good, but the common good. In the case of comprehensive immigration reform, it is completely within the Lutheran tradition to be an advocate for reform that is fair and just as well as protecting the dignity, worth, and value of another child of God. As one lives in the kingdom of the left, a high measure of humility is necessary. As we know ourselves to be sinful, inwardly directed to self against God and neighbor, and far from perfect, our efforts to craft and create proposals, resolutions, and even laws may be wrong.

With regard to the kingdom of the right, which Lutherans herald as the realm of God's saving, redeeming, and reconciling work through Jesus's death and resurrection (the Gospel), wherever one finds oneself on the issue of immigration or immigration reform, there is common ground to be found in God's biblical mandate and Christ's example to welcome the stranger and to love one's neighbor as oneself.

This is a lens by which I seek to lead and advocate. This Lutheran lens is colored by my understanding of the witness of the scriptures and my own cultural upbringing. This lens provides some focus through which I can seek to provide an answer to questions that continues to be raised: "What it is about the word 'illegal' that you don't understand, Bishop?" "Are we as citizens or Christians called to condone those who blatantly violate the law of our land?" "Does such behavior really honor God or reflect what Jesus would do?"

Martin Luther, in speaking of hospitality given to the persecuted and oppressed, said, "God Himself is in our home, is being fed at our house, is lying down and resting."[5] The truth of the matter is that because of a broken immigration system and a lack of will among our national leaders, we have experienced a surge of legislative attempts from statehouses across this country in an effort to take matters into their own hands or to motivate the White House and the Congress to move beyond partisan politics and actually work together to address the need for comprehensive reform. Unfortunately, most of the local legislation includes rhetoric with the potential to dehumanize and harm.

One of my colleagues, Bishop Steven Ullestad of the Northeast Iowa Synod, was invited to attend a state dinner at the White House. As he and his wife went through the reception line to meet the president and Mrs. Obama and other dignitaries, Bishop Ullestad shook the president's hand and introduced himself as being the Lutheran bishop in the territory in which Postville, Iowa, resides, the president assured him that immigration reform was at the top of his agenda.

Postville, Iowa, is in the center of the United States. It is a small town with a meatpacking plant that was actually growing and embracing the immigrants that helped Postville counter the trends of most shrinking small towns in America. Bishop Ullestad describes what happened on May 12, 2008, in Postville:

> May 12 happened and everything changed. That morning, schools and computers were shut down. All the roads into and out of Postville were blockaded by people with guns and guard dogs. Government trucks crashed through the gates of the local meatpacking plant. Hundreds of ICE officers and other police officers with guard dogs

---

5 Quoted in Christine Pohl, *Making Room: Recovering Hospitality as a Christian Tradition*, (Grand Rapids: Eerdmans, 1996), 6.

and guns surrounded the place. Everyone with
a Latino background was brought out in hand-
cuffs, whether documented or undocumented,
while Black Hawk helicopters with machine guns
visible circled overhead. Our little town of 2,300
was in shock. One local pastor described it as an
invasion. The archbishop used the word "terror"
to describe the impact on the community. One
woman asked the question of me, "Why did the
government decide to destroy our town?" I need
to emphasize the number of people—389 individuals arrested in a town of 2,300—that are simply
gone. You can imagine the impact on families,
schools, downtown businesses, and everything
else. Why do this to towns and why do this to
children?[6]

In Arizona, a scene like Postville has not taken place, but
on numerous occasions workplaces and communities have
experienced armed law enforcement officers from the
Maricopa County Sheriff's Office doing what the infamous
Sheriff Joe Arpaio likes to call "sweeping for illegal aliens."
Even though these raids sweep up American citizens along
with those who may be undocumented, the attitude of the
sheriff, with much public support, is "I am simply trying to
enforce laws that the federal government refuses to address."

In light of the current immigration climate in the metro
area where I live, within the state of Arizona and the United
States, I lean not just upon the witness of scripture, the
example of Jesus, and my family's journey along the border,
but I seek to claim the gift of being Lutheran. Lutherans
have a clear sense of being an immigrant church in America.
And that immigrant background has led Lutherans in
America (and around the world) to be intentional about

---

6   Bishop Steven L. Ullestad, comments made in May 2008.

working for justice, practicing mercy, and demonstrating compassion for all of God's children.

One of the gifts Lutherans bring to the table is that of the work of Lutheran Immigration and Refugee Service. When the history of LIRS is reviewed, a reader would find, "For more than seven decades Lutheran Immigration and Refugee Service has been a champion for refugees and migrants from around the globe. Our legacy of courageous and compassionate service has made a difference in the lives of hundreds of thousands of people who have sought safety and hope in America's communities. Our history reflects American Lutherans' deep immigrant roots and passionate commitment to welcoming newcomers."[7] This ministry of the Lutheran faith community began as a response to refugees and displaced people following World War I, formally becoming LIRS in 1939. During World War II, one in six displaced persons was a Lutheran.

The vision of this pan-Lutheran extension of the church is that "all migrants and refugees are protected, embraced, and empowered in a world of just and welcoming communities." And its mission is "witnessing to God's love for all people, we stand with and advocate for migrants and refugees, transforming communities through ministries of service and justice."[8]

Standing with and advocating for migrants and refugees involves speaking for and acting for the sake of the documented and undocumented. Because of this call, the staff of LIRS, the staff of the ELCA Office for Advocacy, along with the ELCA Conference of Bishops has invested much time and energy speaking with elected leaders at state and national levels to petition for comprehensive immigration reform. My experience over the past six years is that it is not politically expedient to address this problem, as it is weighed

---

7   http://lirs.org/our-work/about-us/identityvision-mission/.
8   Ibid.

against other competing issues such as the debt crisis, job recovery, and two wars being fought. In my meetings with congressional members or their staff, I have found both an openness to as well as a complete deflection of Congress's need to fix a long-broken policy. I have listened from one election year to the next that now is not the time, there just is not enough political will to address the whole thing, but maybe some pieces can be passed. Changes in the focus of ICE and the president's recent deferred-action toward undocumented individuals who were brought to the United States as children or teenagers represents some effort at a piecemeal attempt to address the more politically amenable parts of the immigration challenge. But, as witnessed by the leadership of Governor Brewer to deny driver's licenses to those young undocumented immigrants who were able to apply on Wednesday, August 15, 2012, for the new federal program allowing them to stay and work temporarily in the United States, without comprehensive reform, temporary measures can create a sense of false hope. Communities and individuals continue to suffer and live in fear, and state legislatures or governors continue to craft their own responses that seek to supersede the role of the federal government.

In an effort to guide our elected leaders and to inform Lutherans within our faith communities, LIRS has established a position for calling our elected leaders to work for comprehensive immigration reform:[9]

LIRS supports a comprehensive solution to the United States's broken immigration system. LIRS urges Congress and the Obama administration to work collectively to pass and enact into law fair and humane immigration reform legislation.

LIRS advocates for reform that includes the following provisions:

---

9 Material quoted from the position of Lutheran Immigration and Refugee Service per Comprehensive Immigration Reform found at www.lirs.org.

- Provides an earned pathway to lawful permanent residency and eventual citizenship for undocumented immigrants and their families
- Ensures the humane enforcement of U.S. immigration laws, specifically within the immigration detention system to reduce the reliance upon the incarceration of vulnerable immigrants and to promote the use of community-based alternatives-to-detention programs
- Protects families from separation and ensures an adequate supply of visas for families seeking to reunite in order to reduce the long delays currently experienced by immigrants awaiting family reunification
- Ensures the protection of U.S. citizens and immigrant workers
- Provides adequate resources and protections in order to ensure the successful integration of refugees, asylees, unaccompanied minors, and other vulnerable migrant populations.

Supporting the recommendations of Lutheran Immigration and Refugee Service, my own denomination, the Evangelical Lutheran Church in America, issued in 2010 a Social Policy Resolution addressed to our elected national leaders. Within that resolution are five action points:

1. Reunite families and integrate the marginalized
2. Protect the rights of people at work
3. Establish just and humane enforcement
4. Revitalize refugee protection and integration
5. Address root causes of forced migration

Lutherans understand the need for government to govern. Lutherans are invited and encouraged to participate in the process of rising up and electing women and men who have the gifts to lead, again, not just for individual or parochial benefit, but the benefit of all. My denomination has affirmed the right and the need for our nation to secure and control its borders. Though I often hear that those pushing for immigration reform are advocates of open borders, that is not the case, at least from the Lutheran leadership of LIRS or the ELCA. The spiritual and moral challenge is to refute the excuses of border insecurity for avoiding comprehensive immigration reform. Evidence continues to indicate that our borders are more secure and crime rates along the border with Mexico are at an all-time low.[10] To illustrate: currently in the state of Arizona, public fundraising continues to seek to raise resources to pay for a full-fencing of the border. As the November 2012 elections approach, a variety of candidates promise this will be a priority.

I understand this concern regarding border security because I have experienced it firsthand. As I work with ecumenical leaders on this topic, none are advocating for "open borders," though there may be debate and differences on how our country has worked to secure the border. However, if our elected leaders and a number of residents along the border continue to believe that half of the Arizona border remains unsecure, how much needs to be done, and when will the improvements be enough to satisfy those who say the border has to be secure before the nation can pursue comprehensive reform?

According to Pinal County Sheriff Paul Babeau in an April 21, 2011, article in the *Arizona Republic*:

> The border cannot be secured without three key elements of the 10-Point Border Security Plan by Sens. John McCain and Jon Kyl:
>
> Immediately deploy 6,000 armed soldiers for a period of two years. While armed soldiers are deployed, the double-barrier fence should be

---

10 http://www.usatoday.com/news/washington/2011-07-15-border-violence-main_n.htm.

completed with video surveillance, lighting, sensors and roads to support rapid deployment of Border Patrol. Finally, fully enforce the law without any diversion option for illegal immigrants. This plan was implemented in the Yuma Sector, resulting in a 96 percent reduction in illegal border crossings."[11]

The ELCA urges our government to establish just and humane enforcement. The social policy resolution states:

> This church believes that governing authorities have the responsibility to protect the nation's borders and maintain its security. It supports the establishment of clear protocols for raids on worksites and safeguards that ensure immigrant families and local communities are not harmed. It is troubled by the use of criminal charges in routine immigration-status violations and advocates against this approach. The ELCA also supports increasing the use of more humane, less costly, and more effective alternatives to detention, such as supervised release programs. When detention is necessary, compliance with humane standards and access to vital services must be ensured at every facility housing detainees. Families with children should never be detained in penal settings. Children should be united with family members whenever possible or provided with guardianship if needed. Immigrant children in federal custody ought to be treated in accordance with child welfare principles consistent with American values, for example, the right to appointed legal representation and a hearing before a judge. It supports the

11 Paul Babeu, "Focus on Secure Border, Not Illegal-Immigration Amnesty," *The Arizona Republic*, Thursday, April 21, 2011.

right to judicial review and advocates for increased access to legal counsel for immigrants to seek opportunities for relief from detention and deportation. Finally, the ELCA calls for a moratorium on and a comprehensive assessment of fence building along the United States-Mexican border, noting especially its impact on local communities."[12]

Enforcement issues appear to dominate the immigration debate with little room for the issue of reform itself. It is easy to be confused by all the banter that takes place and the distrust of the evidence presented. In the meantime, we still have 11 to 12 million undocumented residents living in the shadows of our neighborhoods. Many are related to U.S. citizens and many are children who were brought across the border as infants or small children.

President Obama's "deferred-action" program seeks to speak to the so-called "Dreamers" dwelling in our midst. Such is the story of Angelica Hernandez. Terry Greene Sterling tells Angelica's story in her June 30, 2011, column in the *Arizona Republic*, "Top Student Pins Her Hopes on Dream Act." In May 2011, Angelica graduated summa cum laude from Arizona State University's Ira Fulton School of Engineering. She was named outstanding Senior in Mechanical Engineering. On June 28, 2011, she joined other unauthorized-immigrant academic superstars at a senate judiciary committee hearing in Washington, D.C. The topic of the hearing was the Dream Act, proposed legislation that would give temporary legal residency to young noncriminal unauthorized immigrants like Angelica who were brought to the United States illegally as kids. The Dream Act would allow them to serve in the military and attend college. If they fulfilled their obligations, they'd get in a seven-year

12   ELCA Social Policy Resolution "Toward Compassionate, Just, and Wise Immigration Reform," 2010.

line for citizenship. They'd pay taxes, ramp up the military, and bolster the professional middle class.[13]

Because all attempts to pass the Dream Act over the past ten years have failed, whether it was wrapped into a comprehensive immigration reform measure or because it is perceived as "backdoor amnesty,"[14]—our neighbors like Angelica live in a sort of limbo. Though she has recognized gifts and abilities, she is not entitled to work in this country. It is hoped that the president's action, though condemned by some as a scandalous use of his executive powers, will provide some breathing space to continue the work needed for comprehensive and just immigration reform.

Somewhere in this conversation, phrases like "an earned pathway" or "backdoor amnesty" have to be addressed. Our culture has become attuned to certain buzzwords around certain topics. Such words elevate emotions, impede debate, and ultimately derail productive progress on difficult and complex topics. Much energy has to be devoted to clarifying and amplifying what is meant or not meant by particular words. As a Lutheran leader living and serving along the border, let me be clear that LIRS and the ELCA do not advocate for amnesty. In this case, I understand amnesty as a general overlooking or pardon of past offenses by the government. Those who oppose creating any means by which the undocumented may remain in our country point to 1986, when President Ronald Reagan led the way for 3 million undocumented residents to become legal residents. Following this action, there was a surge in undocumented residents into the United States. However, like past increases in undocumented workers coming into this country, the demand of a growing economy in the United States and the lack of development and political instability

---

13 Terry Greene Sterling, "Top Student Pins Her Hopes on Dream Act," *Arizona Republic*, Thursday, June 30, 2011.

14 Ibid.

in Mexico and Central America are seen as the primary drivers for the increase in numbers, and not amnesty itself.

LIRS and the ELCA do not endorse or support amnesty in any form with regard to comprehensive immigration reform. There is a clear understanding that there is a large backlog of individuals who have sought to work within the confines of the current system and that these persons need to be processed before those who find themselves residing in this country without proper documentation. However, our church advocates for the sheer number of undocumented people, many interconnected to families who are here legally. Immigration reform needs to provide a way for those out of status to make amends and earn legal status in this country.

In the fall of 2009, I sat with a small group of ELCA bishops in the office of Illinois Representative Luis Gutierrez in Washington, D.C. Representative Gutierrez clearly knew that any legislation pertaining to comprehensive immigration reform was a long shot, but he wanted this issue to remain before his fellow lawmakers. So in December 2009, Congressman Gutierrez introduced an immigration bill that would allow undocumented immigrants who have contributed to the United States through work, study, military, or community service to pay a fine and pass a background check to obtain a conditional legal residence. They would then have to wait a full six years before applying for a green card, during which time they would continue to contribute to the United States, pay taxes, remain crime free, learn English, and meet certain civic requirements. The requirements were an attempt to remove the label that any attempt to allow undocumented residents to stay in this country was simply "amnesty" that, based on the experience during the Reagan years, just encourages more people to come into our country through illegal channels.

The debate over "secure borders" and "earned pathway" is only going to escalate. There is cautious optimism that there just might be a political will to move on the issue of comprehensive immigration reform. Following the outcome of the November 2012 elections, there has been a surge in reengaging the conversation, not just about pieces of reform, but very intentional actions. Advocates and critics are encouraged or challenged by the forming of a bipartisan committee of Senators, including McCain and Flake from Arizona, who are floating possible legislation. In light of how the Latino block of voters responded in the election, there appears to be a new will to create a tough but fair path to citizenship. That path would be contingent on securing our borders, as well as tracking legal immigrants; it includes reforming the system to strengthen the economy and American families, the creation of an effective employment verification system to address issues of identity theft, and an improvement in the process to allow in those workers essential to our economy while providing protection for existing workers.

Yes, our leaders, and maybe even our fellow citizens, will have to find common ground on how secure a border must be and our national will to allow those living in the shadows an opportunity to live legally and openly. Putting a human face on this issue can help soften some of the rhetoric. Unfortunately, for many, the undocumented in our midst still remain invisible—or those who happen to look Latino all get lumped into a single category. As a spiritual leader, I am called to help remind others that any human being is a child of God, uniquely and lovingly created by our compassionate creator. When I worship or gather with our Latino Lutheran sisters and brothers, I sense a passion for God, a commitment to community, and an empathy for the stranger in their midst. All of our Latino congregations present a younger demographic than our Anglo congregations.

If demographers are correct, members of the Latino community will be the majority population in Arizona within a generation. If the Lutheran Church wants to have a future in this area of the country, then those in the congregations of this synod have to work to cross the barriers that our fear, ignorance, and sense of entitlement erect. Right now in our congregations and mission developments are young Christian Lutherans who love the Lord and love the church, but they happen to be born to undocumented parents or were brought here as small children. They question why they are seen as such a threat or wonder if people would still hate them if they got to know them.

My first call as a pastor was to serve the people of faith at American Evangelical Lutheran Church, Tucson, Arizona. In 1985 three elementary-age children joined the community. They came to stay with their aunt, escaping the conflict that had erupted into civil war in El Salvador. They did not have appropriate papers or documentation. Their mother had died of cancer and they had witnessed their father, a military officer, be assassinated. Through the network of family relationships, the children made it to Tucson. This was pre-9/11, so their aunt, a U.S. citizen, was able to escort them across the border without any questions being asked. At one point, because they had not been processed correctly or granted asylum, there was grave concern that they would be deported back to El Salvador, where they could have been potential targets to those who opposed their father.

It must be pointed out that an assessment of this congregation would indicate the members of American to be fairly conservative theologically and politically. The congregation was 99 percent Anglo, mostly Midwestern transplants, and a sizable number of people near or at retirement age. This was not a group noted for their activism. As the drama of the Yanez children played out before the eyes of the congregation, it was amazing to see how many embraced these children, who came to them as strangers, but now were perceived as part of their faith family. When a court hearing was called, dozens of these followers of Jesus crowded the hearing room to let the judge know there was a community that believed in obedience to God and country, understanding that sometimes the letter of the law needs to be placed under the law of love.

In the conversations and debates around what to do with the undocumented living among us, Bible verses are often bantered about. The Apostle Paul's writing to the Christians in Rome often gets thrown into the arena:

> Let every person be subject to the governing authorities; for there is no authority except from God, and those authorities that exist have been instituted by God. Therefore whoever resists authority resists what God has appointed, and those who resist will incur judgment. For rulers are not a terror to good conduct, but to bad. Do you wish to have no fear of the authority? Then do what is good, and you will receive its approval; for it is God's servant for your good. But if you do what is wrong, you should be afraid, for the authority does not bear the sword in vain! It is the servant of God to execute wrath on the wrongdoer. Therefore one must be subject, not only because of wrath but also because of conscience. For the same reason you also pay taxes, for the authorities are God's servants, busy with this very thing. Pay to all what is due to them—taxes to whom taxes are due, revenue to whom revenue is due, respect to whom respect is due, honor to whom honor is due. (Romans 13:1–7)

This passage affirms civil obedience to the authority of the government. Government is seen as established by God for the common good. However, in acknowledging the value and good that government can do, the Christian is guided by a higher law that often gets short shrift; it follows the verses above: "Owe no one anything, except to love one

another; for the one who loves another has fulfilled the law"
(Romans 13:8).

Like Jesus's lesson that upon the love of God and love of
neighbor as oneself hangs or fulfills all the laws, Paul ele-
vates the law of love above the law of the civil or political
authorities.

About fifteen years ago, a parishioner in my congregation started a residential landscape business. He was seventy
years old at the time, but loved working outdoors. Because
of his age and personality, and because he was an English-
speaking Anglo, he began to have more work than he could
manage. As the demand for his services expanded, a Latino
young man was referred to him. José was undocumented,
but married to an American and had two American children. He and his wife even owned a home. Prior to 9/11,
José followed a traditional pattern of migrating back to his
family's ranch in northern Mexico to stay for several weeks
each winter. He managed to get across the border with no
real difficulties, but the climate along the border changed
after our country was attacked. José knew he needed to
gain legal residency. He met with an immigration attorney,
he collected necessary documents, and then he was told
he must return to Mexico, secure a Mexican passport, and
then they could begin to process his application. When he
arrived at the border, all of his papers were taken and he
was informed that because he had entered the country illegally, he was now banned from entering this country for a
minimum of ten years. Maybe José got bad advice, maybe he
did not fully understand all that was involved, but what he
did know was that he had a wife and two children living in
Phoenix who needed him. What advice would you give José?
What would you tell his wife and children, who watched him
play by the rules? What would you do if you found yourself
in that situation? How is the faith community to respond to
José or to his family?

Now the law is very clear about José's situation. He first came into this country without documentation and now must suffer the consequences, which include a ten-year ban from entering the United States while taking his turn in line with all the other Mexican residents seeking legal residency. José chose to take the path that continues to be taken when the hope and the possibility of ever receiving legal residency vanishes. He made his way back across the border, knowing that if he ever is caught again, he will be banned forever! José took that risk, because the law of love supersedes any other law. His love for his wife and his children meant doing whatever it might take to get back to them, even if he got caught or, worse, died due to the harsh elements of the desert environment or at the hands of the various traffickers at work along the border.

At the beginning of this chapter, I spoke about the biblical mandate and my personal connection to life along the border. I think about my maternal grandfather whose religious roots connected him to the Quakers. The Quakers have never been a dominant Christian group in the United States, but their historical witness has been that of being people of peace, respectful of others. Many Quakers engaged in advocacy and worked for changing what they believed to be the unjust and morally wrong system of slavery. Perhaps Quaker involvement in what became the Underground Railroad has something to teach those of us engaged in the immigration struggle:

> Some Quakers participated in loosely organized Underground Railroad networks. A few made the Underground Railroad their life's work. Others may have been willing to aid a fugitive, but the opportunity to do so seldom or never arose. Some abolitionists, including some Quaker abolitionists, felt as a matter of tactics that efforts to end slavery as a system, freeing millions, was better than

providing assistance to the handful of people who freed themselves by escape. These too were likely to aid the individual escaping, but remained apart from the Underground Railroad system.

Not all Quakers, and probably a minority of Quakers, participated in the organized antislavery movement. Some feared that too much association with the "world's people" would compromise Quaker testimonies; others felt that the tactics of some in the anti-slavery movement hindered rather than aided the work of emancipation. This is true. It is equally true that Quakers were represented in the organized anti-slavery movement far in excess of their proportion of the population at large."[15]

What I appreciate in this snippet from history is the tension within a faith community as they struggle to address a complex moral, spiritual, and national issue. Even among the people of peace, there were different viewpoints and paths of engagement. I would say the same is true within the family of faith in which I serve and possibly even within the extended family of which I am member. Voting Arizonans popularly supported the passing of SB 1070. Within the ELCA congregations in Arizona, I have reflected some of the diversity of opinions and experiences. I continue to affirm what my denomination and our partner in Lutheran Immigration and Refugee Service have been advocating. In spite of diverse views and rather than piecemeal attempts to fix a broken system, our elected federal leaders need to address a problem that sits under their responsibility.

In the meantime, I will continue to encourage that we don't lose sight of the other, whichever side the "other" may

---

15   Christopher Densmore, "Quakers and the Underground Railroad: Myths and Realities," http://trilogy.brynmawr.edu/speccoll/quakersandslavery/commentary/organizations/underground_railroad.php.

be in the immigration debate or conversation. In February 2010, I was privileged to travel to our companion synod church in Senegal, West Africa. Senegal is a country that is 90 percent Muslim, 5 percent Christian, and 5 percent other. Since Senegal's independence from colonialism in the 1950s, the crafters of their national constitution made sure that freedom of religion was a key article. Over the past fifty years, religious violence has basically been nonexistent. The country has been served by both Muslim and Christian presidents. I asked one of our Senegalese hosts why it is that other countries, with one religion so dominant to others, have minority groups that are often persecuted or closed out of the political process, when this is not the case in Senegal.

The answer offered was, "We practice cousinery." I queried, "Cousinery? What is cousinery?" His answer was, "Cousinery is the understanding that before I was a Muslim and before you were a Christian, or before you were a part of the Wolof tribe and I was part of the Pulaar tribe, we were cousins. Because we are cousins, we have an obligation as fellow family members to look out for your welfare."

As we address the concerns of the undocumented who live within our midst, I can't help but remember, "We are all cousins, and because we are cousins we have an obligation as fellow family members to look out for your welfare." To look out can mean many things, but as a Christian, I know it means to love my neighbor as myself and to wrestle with who my neighbor is and how I am being neighbor to him or her.

I journey ahead with a sense of hope and humility, which can be a real testimony and gift in light of the attitudes and emotions surrounding this issue. I seek to learn from others, like Julie Erfle. *Arizona Republic* columnist E. J. Montini writes:

> On September 18, 2007, Erfle became a major stakeholder on the immigration and border-security issue when her husband, Nick, a Phoenix

police officer, was killed by an illegal immigrant. Erfle became even more of a stakeholder when she was publicly vilified by a conservative talk show host for opposing Arizona's controversial immigration-enforcement law known as Senate Bill 1070. Supporters of SB 1070 had tried to use Officer Erfle's murder as a clarion call to promote passage of the law. Julie disagreed, and spoke out against them. For that she was attacked on the radio.

As she later explained in an essay for the *Arizona Republic*:

As the surviving spouse of Phoenix police officer Nick Erfle and the mother of his sons, I feel it is my right and, more importantly, my responsibility, to ensure that his memory is used in ways that are consistent with who he was and the values to which he adhered. And so, when I see my husband being used as the poster child for a policy he would not have agreed with, I feel it is my duty to speak out on his behalf.

Regarding the challenge of comprehensive immigration reform, Erfle told me, "Compromise is not a dirty word. We need to be humble enough to realize that we don't have all the answers, and there is room for the other side to make their argument."[16]

My prayer is that after we listen to one another, we still can find a path through this problem that respects the dignity of the other and commits to resolve this problem that will not become any less complex by our procrastination or polarization of our brothers and sisters in Christ.

---

16 E. J. Montini, "Website Helps Officer's Widow Find Her Voice," *Arizona Republic*, April 24, 2011.